Through Children's Eyes
52 Worship Talks for Children

Ben F. Freudenburg

CPH
SAINT LOUIS

I give thanks for Jennifer, my wife, whose patience, love, constant encouragement, support, and hours of dedicated time enabled this writing. And thanks to Cori and Sara, my daughters, who often took time to help make items, assist in the delivery of messages, and lend me their eyes to look through. **Through Children's Eyes** *is dedicated to the many children who have taught me about my Savior Jesus Christ and His love, as they allowed me to look through their eyes.*

Unless otherwise noted, Scripture quotations are taken from the HOLY BIBLE, NEW INTERNATIONAL VERSION®. Copyright © 1973, 1978, 1984 by the International Bible Society. Used by permission of Zondervan Publishing House. All rights reserved.

The "NIV" and "New International Version" trademarks are registered in the United States Patent and Trademark Office by the International Bible Society. Use of either trademark requires the permission of the International Bible Society.

As You Begin is adapted from "The Children's Message: One Step Toward a Child-Friendly Worship," *Lutheran Education,* March/April 1995. *A Friend for Life Who Builds Us Up, A Friend for Life Who Changes Us,* and *A Friend for Life Who Saves* were originally prepared for Friendship Sunday 1995, Board for Evangelism Services, The Lutheran Church Missouri Synod. *Guess Who* was originally prepared for *The Concordia Pulpit,* Concordia Publishing House, 1992.

Copyright © 1996 Ben F. Freudenburg

Published by Concordia Publishing House
3558 S. Jefferson Avenue, St. Louis, MO 63118-3968
Manufactured in the United States of America

Library of Congress Cataloging-in-Publication Data

Freudenburg, Ben F., 1950–

    Through children's eyes: 52 worship talks for children / Ben F. Freudenburg.
       p.   cm.
     ISBN 0-570-04843-5
     1. Children's sermons. 2. Sermons, American. I. Title.
BV4315.F74   1996   95-53701
252´.53—dc20   CIP

1 2 3 4 5 6 7 8 9 10   05 04 03 02 01 00 99 98 97 96

Contents

Seasonal Talks

Patterns

As You Begin

The Children's Message

Children belong in worship. They are a part of the family of God. How many of us learned the words of the Lord's Prayer or the Apostles' Creed in worship? Learned how to confess our sin or forgive the sin of others? How many of us developed our pictures of God through the words, symbols, songs, music, and liturgy of worship? The Holy Spirit shapes our faith and our sense of God in worship.

The children's message belongs in every gathering for corporate worship. Presenting a message each week says to children, "You are an important part of the family of God. You are so important that we always arrange our worship to include you."

Early childhood years—ages 2 through 8—are highly important years for faith development. Including children in worship in special ways will help them value worship throughout their lives. The children's message is one of the best ways to make your worship child-friendly.

Some Children's Messages Do's

1. Do write it out. Please don't wing it. It is an important part of worship and should be prepared with as much care as the sermon for adults or the anthem of the choir.

2. Do memorize it. Your talk should be about seven minutes long. Please don't read it. Memorizing it keeps you from rambling on and on. It will give you confidence and help you stay on track when a child responds with a great line.

3. Do practice it. What works in one's head or on paper doesn't always work at the altar. Practicing will help you get the bugs out and allow you to be relaxed. A natural presentation keeps the children focused on what you are saying.

4. Do anticipate the movement and response of the children. If you bring in a lighted Christmas tree, expect that young children will want to touch it. If you offer a child a cookie and have none for the others, expect some children to be sad, and even cry.

5. Do build your message around only one point or truth. In seven minutes, you will only have time to make one point. One spiritual truth is all the children will remember anyway. Ask the Holy Spirit's guidance in drawing the one truth from Scripture that God asks you to teach His children. Do a great job of communicating that truth to the children. Do keep it simple.

6. Do involve the children. But don't let them get out of control. Involve the children through sight, sound, smell, taste, touch, action, singing, answering questions, and assisting you.

7. Do experiment, have fun, celebrate!

8. Do keep the message and the vocabulary age-appropriate. But don't always aim at the youngest. Aim your language and message at different age-levels on different Sundays.

9. Do invite children into God's presence and help them sense His wonder. Children won't always understand everything you say, but they will sense God's wonder, might, and glory.

10. Do include directions for your congregation. You may want to print directions in your bulletin that the children may come forward during the first stanzas of a hymn, then return to their seats as the congregation sings the last stanzas. Whether you print directions or invite the children up yourself, include the age range of children you are involving.

11. Do use handouts and objects to reinforce the message at home. Ask helpers to hand out the take-home items as the children leave. This will give you time to remove your props so worship can continue.

12. Most importantly—do include the Gospel in every lesson. Don't assume that each child knows the love of God through Jesus Christ. And don't turn the Gospel into work-righteous actions: "Jesus loves you if you do this or that." That is not Gospel. Jesus loves us unconditionally. He proved it by dying on the cross to pay for our sins, and by rising from the dead on Easter Sunday. Jesus loves us—even when we are bad. He helps us live out our response to His love by loving others.

Gifts to Live By

Truth to Teach: God gives us His Ten Commandments to help us love Him and one another.

Scripture: Exodus 20:1–17

Preparation: Number cards from 1 to 10. Write the matching statement below on each card. On the back of each card, write the letter enclosed in parentheses. Wrap the cards in a gift box. Attach a tag reading: To: The Children of God; From: God the Father. Hide the box in a bag. Duplicate the 10 rules (without the ending letter) on card stock so that each child may take a copy home. Place a self-adhesive magnetic strip (available at hardware and craft stores) on the back of each copy.

God's Rules—Our Gifts to Live By

1. Love God and keep Him first. (G)
2. Keep God's name holy. (O)
3. Worship God regularly. (D)
4. Obey parents and others in authority. (')
5. No killing. (S)
6. Respect the gift of sexuality. (R)
7. No stealing. (U)
8. Don't hurt anyone's reputation. (L)
9. Don't covet other's stuff. (E)
10. Don't covet people or their gifts. (S)

Hide the gift-wrapped box in a bag as you greet the children.

(Carrying bag) Boys and girls, it's so great to see you this morning. Would you pray with me? I'll say a few words, and you repeat those words after me. May the words/of my mouth/and the feelings/of my heart/be what You want,/Jesus./Amen.

You know what? I feel like Santa Claus! It's because I have a bag with a gift in it. Would you like to see what the gift is? *Ask children to help you pull out the gift and read the tag.*

Ask the children to help you open the box and pull out the cards. What kind of gift is this? Maybe we have to look at each part of the gift. *Ask 10 children to each hold a card, standing so that the numerals face the congregation.*

Let's read what the cards say. *Read each of the rules. Then ask children if they recognize the gift.* Let's see if you're right. *Ask children to turn the cards around.* You're right! These cards do tell us about the Ten Commandments—God's rules.

God's rules are a great gift. Why do you think He gave them to us? That's right, God loves us so much that He wants us to keep safe, and know how to share His love. The more I learn about God's rules, the more I see how good they are for me. But what if I break one of these rules and get into big trouble? Will God stop loving me?

Of course not. God sent His own Son Jesus to keep these rules perfectly. He let Jesus die on a cross and rise again so that we can be forgiven when we break the rules.

Boys and girls, get to know your gift—God's Rules. Ask Jesus to help you understand them and follow them. As you go back to your seat, take my gift with you. You can hang God's Rules on your refrigerator and talk about how Jesus will help your family keep them.

Is God Calling Me to Work in His Church?

Truth to Teach: God helps us answer His call to serve in His church.

Scripture: 1 Samuel 3:1–10

Preparation: Music baton; hymnal; chalkboard eraser; chalk; pastor's stole; Bible; Sunday school, vacation Bible school, or youth group materials. You may wish to use this message as the Old Testament lesson is read.

Listen very closely while I read you a story from God's Word. Then I'll ask you some questions about it. *Read 1 Samuel 3:1–10.*

Now, are you ready for the questions? Who was being called in the middle of his sleep? *Give children time to respond to each question.* Who did Samuel think was calling him? Who was really calling him? Why was God calling Samuel? *Let children respond.*

Can you believe it? God was calling a little boy—a child—to serve Him! Did you know that God calls you to serve Him too? Maybe He is even calling you to be a full-time worker in the church.

Ask a child to hold the baton and hymnal. God might be calling you to be a minister of music. You can lead the song of the church, like *(name your music director).*

Ask another child to hold up the teaching tools. Or God might call you to be a teaching minister in a Christian school. *If you work in partnership with a day school, or if there is a Christian school in your area, name a teacher the children might know.*

Hold up the stole and Bible. God might call you to be a missionary or a pastor, like *(name your pastor).*

(Hold up the Sunday school, vacation Bible school, or youth ministry items.) Or God might call you to be a director of Christian education, like *(name the person in that position.)*

Boys and girls, God needs full-time workers in His church. He wants everyone in the world to know that He sent His own Son Jesus to die in their place, and rise again to win them eternal life. You can tell that good news right now.

But keep listening! God just may be calling you to serve Him full-time in His church!

The Good Shepherd

Truth to Teach: Jesus loves us and keeps us safe, just as a loving shepherd protects his sheep.

Scripture: Psalm 23, John 10:11–15

Preparation: Cut a shepherd's staff from cardboard or Foamboard. Use a paper fastener to attach a cross piece that can swivel out from behind the staff to form a cross. Wolf mask. (You may want to have an adult appear at the right time, wearing the mask, but be sure small children aren't frightened.) Copy Psalm 23 on cardstock, so each child may have a card to take home.

Boys and girls, are you lambs? Of course not! You are children. But did you know that Jesus calls His children "lambs"? We even sing a song about it. *Sing "I Am Jesus' Little Lamb" with the children.*

If we are lambs, who is our Good Shepherd? That's right. In John 10:11, Jesus says, "I am the Good Shepherd."

Most of us don't really know much about lambs and shepherds. Let's see if we can't learn something about them. Pretend you are lambs. What sound do lambs make? *Let the children b-a-a-a.* That's absolutely right. Okay, lambs, let's hear it—where do lambs live? That's right, in a field, or on a hillside, where the grass is green.

What would lambs be doing in the field or on the hillside? Yes, they would eat and play and nap. Go ahead—eat and play and nap. Be lambs!

Wait a minute! Who would be watching over the lambs? That's right, the good shepherd would. *Point the staff at several children.* Hey, you lambs over there, Fluffy and Muffy, don't eat too much or you'll get sick. You two, Scruffy and Crewcut, mind your manners!

You see, boys and girls, the good shepherd knows his lambs by name, and the lambs listen to the good shepherd's voice and obey him.

Lambs, come real close. You must be on your guard, for the mean wolf would like to eat you for his supper. In fact, there is one now! *Show mask or let wolf appear. If small children are frightened, show them immediately that the wolf is pretend.* The good shepherd *(stand up and pretend to protect the lambs)* would protect the lambs from the wolf. He would fight the wolf off, even if it meant dying for the lambs.

Boys and girls, Jesus, our Good Shepherd, is our protector. Jesus protects us from the devil and his evil. In fact, Jesus defeated the devil once and for all *(swivel out the cross piece)* by dying on the cross for us. He loves us so much, He gave His life for us. Then God showed the devil who was boss by raising Jesus from the dead on Easter morning.

Psalm 23 tells us how our Good Shepherd takes care of us. Take a card with you and read Psalm 23 with your family tonight. And have a good day in the safe arms of Jesus, our Good Shepherd. *Distribute cards as children leave.*

The Quake Calmer

Truth to Teach: Jesus is always with us to calm our fears.

Scripture: Psalm 46

Preparation: Assemble an Earthquake Kit. Fill a box with a bottle of water, food items, flashlight, first-aid supplies, radio and batteries, and a blanket. Make copies of the pictures of a heart, angel, cross, and rainbow on page 62, and place them in the box. Be ready to tape or glue them on the four sides of the box. Duplicate copies of the page so each child can take one home. (If children in your area aren't familiar with earthquakes, talk about another type of natural disaster or storm they have experienced, or heard about on the news.)

How many of you have heard some talk about earthquakes? Tell me what you've heard. *Discuss the probablity of having an earthquake and what it might be like.* How does all this earthquake talk make you feel? *Be sure young children don't become frightened.*

Boys and girls, I don't know if we'll have an earthquake or not. But it's a good idea to be prepared, so I've put together an Earthquake Kit. First, *(pull out the heart)* I have a heart. *Tape heart to side of box.* This is to remind me that Jesus loves me so much, that He promises to always be with me. Jesus is my Quake Calmer. Can you say that? Say it after me. Jesus is my Quake Calmer.

In my box I also have *(take out items)* water and food, and an *(let children identify the angel).* That's right. Jesus sends His angels to guard and protect us. Even though we can't see them, they are all around us, keeping us safe. Do you know why Jesus sends the angels to help us? Because Jesus is my Quake Calmer. *Ask children to repeat the phrase.* There is a prayer written around this angel. Let me read it to you. *Read the prayer written around the angel figure.*

In my box I also have a flashlight, first-aid kit, and a *(let children identify the cross; attach it to box).* The cross reminds me that Jesus died for me to take the punishment for my sin, and rose again on Easter. He gave me faith at my Baptism, so I can believe in Him. If I die, I will live forever with Jesus in heaven. I don't have to be afraid of death. Jesus is my Quake Calmer. *Repeat.*

Let's see, I still have a radio and batteries in here, and a blanket, and *(let children identify rainbow; attach it to box).* That's right, a rainbow, to remind me that all God's promises are true.

Whether it is a snowstorm, a tornado, an earthquake, or just a bad day at school, *(show heart)* Jesus stays right by me and loves me. *Show angel.* Jesus sends His angels to guard and guide me. *Show cross.* Jesus died and rose from the dead, so even sin, death, and the devil can't hurt me. *Show rainbow.* All God's promises are true. Jesus is my Quake Calmer.

Take these pictures home today and make your own Quake Calmer Kit. Keep it where you and your family can see it and remember, Jesus is my Quake Calmer. *Hand out pictures.*

Hercomer

Truth to Teach: God created you. You are fearfully and wonderfully made.

Scripture: Psalm 139:14

Preparation: Purchase an "I am special" sticker for each child, or write that statement on a self-adhesive tag for each child. Prepare an adult to play "Hercomer's" role. He will be dressed shabbily and sitting in the congregation. In a bag, place an orange, a potted plant, and a teddy bear. Have an empty chair close by.

Leader: Boys and girls, God created so many wonderful things for us to enjoy. In my bag, I have some different things that God created. I'll hold up an item from the bag, and you say what it is. Then I'll say, "And God said…." And you (and the whole congregation) will say "It is good."

Let's try it. God created *(hold up orange and let children respond.)* And God said, *(let children and congregation respond "It is good"). Repeat with potted plant. Then say,* God gave workers the skill and materials to make a *(repeat with teddy bear).*

Hercomer stands up in congregation and starts to leave. Engage him in the following dialog.

Leader: Sir, your name is Hercomer, isn't it?

Hercomer: Yes *(shyly).*

Leader: Why are you leaving?

Hercomer: Well, I guess I don't really fit in.

Leader: Come here, Hercomer. What do you mean, you don't fit in?

Hercomer: I'm not good.

Leader: What do you mean? God made all things good—and He made you!

Hercomer: Look at my clothes. Everybody is dressed better than me. I'm no good.

Leader *(to children)*: Boys and girls, do clothes make Hercomer good? *Let children respond.*

Hercomer: But I live in one room. Good people have nice big homes.

Leader: Boys and girls, does living in a house make you good?

Hercomer: Nobody really loves me. I just don't fit in.

Leader: I know how to convince him. *Invite Hercomer to sit in the chair in the midst of the children. Point to him and say,* Boys and girls, God created *(let children fill in words: Hercomer)* and He said, he is *(good.)*

See what I mean, Hercomer? God doesn't love us or call us good because we have nice clothes or a big house. He loves us because He created us. He gave us life. He thinks we are so special that He sent His own Son, Jesus, to die in our place and rise again. God loves you, no matter what, Hercomer. And you do fit in here. Boys and girls, who will give Hercomer a hug?

Boys and girls, God created each one of you in a wonderful way. You are special to God. Wear an "I-am-special" sticker today to remind you how wonderfully God created you. *Hug Hercomer and give him a sticker as well.*

It's a Baby! It's Life!

Truth to Teach: God values life and knows and loves each one of us, even while in our mother's womb.

Scripture: Jeremiah 1:4–5

Preparation: Invite a woman who is pregnant to help you during the talk. You may wish to order "The Young One," a small plastic doll the size of a fetus at 11–12 weeks for each child. (Project "Young One," Inc., 2125 West Lawn Ave., Racine, WI 53405.)

Boys and girls, I'd like you to meet *(name of mother who is helping)*. She has had some changes in her life in the last few months. Can anyone tell me what's changed? That's right, she is going to have a baby.

The baby growing inside *(name of helper)* is alive. It is real. In fact, after growing inside its mother for only 11 weeks, a baby is this big. *Show fetus model, or hold fingers two inches apart.*

Do any of you know, by looking at *(name of helper)*, if the baby is a boy or a girl? *Let the children predict the baby's sex, but point out that they can't know for sure just by looking.* Do you know the color of the baby's eyes? Or the color of its hair? No, we don't know; but there is Someone who knows. It is the same Someone who knew all about you and me as we were growing inside our mothers.

Who knows what this baby is like? God knows! God knew all about you and what you would be like, before you were even born. He made each of you special. Raise your hand if you have blue eyes. Brown hair. Green eyes. Blonde hair. Brown eyes. If you play baseball. If you sing in the choir. If you like to chew gum.

God knew all those things about you, even while you were still living inside your mother. More important, He loved you as His own child. He let His own Son Jesus die to pay for your sins. He planned for your parents to bring you to be baptized and learn about Jesus, so you can believe in Him and live in heaven one day.

God loves you now, just as much as He loved you when you were growing inside your mom. He has special plans for you to serve Him. Isn't it great to be alive—and to belong to God! Repeat our prayer after me. Dear God,/Thank You for making me,/for giving me hair and eyes,/love and life./Be with *(name of helper)*/and the baby./Thank You for all babies./In Jesus' name. Amen. *Hand out dolls as children leave.*

The Three T's of Temptation

Truth to Teach: Jesus is with us to help us say no to temptation, and has earned forgiveness for us when we fail.

Scripture: Matthew 4:1–11

Preparation: Fill a large jar with candy. Print the word *TempTaTion* on a banner or poster, making the T's stand out boldly.

Boys and girls, the word for today is "temptation." *Ask two children to hold up the sign for you.* In the Lord's Prayer we pray, "Lead us not into temptation."

Temptation is the devil's tricky way of getting us to sin. He tempts us to do things when we have been told "no," but we want to do it anyway. Let's learn about the three T's *(point to the T's on the sign)* of temptation.

Hold up the candy jar. Mom says, "No candy before supper." Then she sets the jar on the shelf. I sit there and look at the jar full of candy. It looks so good. Boy, I'd like a piece, how about you? But Mom said no! *(Point to the first T.)* The first T in temptation is the temptation itself.

I start to walk away, but then this little voice in my head tries to trick me! It says, "*(your name)*, it's okay. Nobody is looking. There must be 200 pieces of candy in that jar. Nobody will know one is missing. Take one!"

I start to reach into the jar, but then I say, "No!" But that little voice says, "You'll get one after supper, anyway. Take one now and don't take one after supper. That will even it out!"

Point to the second T. That's the second T in temptation—the trick. Satan tries to trick us into believing it's okay to do the very thing we aren't supposed to do. Raise your hand if that has ever happened to you. *Raise your hand.* Me too!

Point to the last T. Now comes the hardest T of temptation—the test. Will I say "No," not give in and sin, and not take the candy? Or will I say "Yes," give in and sin, and take the candy?

This last T can seem very hard when we feel we have to pass the temptation test on our own. But listen carefully—We are not alone. Jesus is always with us to help us when we are tempted. He gives us the courage to say no and walk away! And because He died on the cross to take the punishment for our sins, He promises to forgive us when we fail, and helps us to do better the next time.

I'm going to keep the candy in the jar today to remind us that, with Jesus' help, we can say no to *(point to the word)* temptation. *Place the candy jar on the altar for the rest of the service so the children will be able to see it.*

Be Salt

Truth to Teach: Through His redeeming sacrifice on the cross, Jesus enables us to be the salt of the earth and make things better.

Scripture: Matthew 5:13

Preparation: Have a popcorn popper, apron, and ingredients ready to make popcorn. Have a large bowl and a large salt shaker handy. Get salt packets from a fast-food restaurant and mark them with crosses.

Start popping popcorn as the children come forward. Ask one child to be the "popcorn watcher." Put the apron on him. (If making popcorn isn't feasible, have some ready-made.)

Boys and girls, it's great to see you in church this morning. Listen to Jesus' words from Matthew 5:13, "You are the salt of the earth." Jesus means, as we share His love, we can make the world a better place.

Let me show you what I mean. *Turn to popcorn watcher.* Is the popcorn ready? Good. I need another volunteer. *Give a volunteer a bowl of unsalted popcorn and ask him/her to taste it.* How does it taste? What is missing? *Lead the child to say that the popcorn is missing salt. Then salt the popcorn and ask the child to taste it again.* How does it taste now? What made it better?

Salt did its job. It made the popcorn taste better. Jesus makes things better too. Think of the time when Jesus was in a boat with His disciples and a big storm came up. What did Jesus do to make it better? *Let children respond.* Yes, He calmed the storm.

When Jesus saw a blind man by the side of the road, what did He do to make the blind man better? *Let children respond.* That's right. He helped the man to see.

We are full of sin and can't get to heaven on our own. What did Jesus do to make it better? That's right. Jesus died on the cross to take away our sin, and rose on Easter to win us life with Him. That's what Jesus did to make our lives better. He helps us to share His love and the Good News about what He has done for us. That's why He tells us we are the salt of the earth—we can help make the world a better place.

When you see someone who is hungry, how can you make things better? *Let children respond. In each case, lead the children to see how Jesus will help them respond in Christian love. Include the power of prayer as something we can do to help others, and explain that it is Jesus working in us that allows us to do good things.* When you see someone who is sick, how can you make things better? When you see people whose homes have been destroyed, what can you do to make things better? If you see someone who doesn't know Jesus, what can you do to make it better?

As you go back to your seat, remember, you are the salt of the earth. Jesus will help you make things better. *Give each child a salt packet marked with a cross.*

So-o-o Big!

Truth to Teach: God's love is so-o-o big, He answers our prayers and helps us in every situation.

Scripture: Matthew 7:7; Exodus 3:1—4:17

Preparation: You may want to give each child a bookmark with the text of Matthew 7:7 printed on it, or give each child a storybook about Moses, such as *Moses and the Freedom Flight,* order no. 59-1478, Concordia Publishing House.

Boys and girls, I know a game parents sometimes play with their babies. They say, "How big are you?" The baby raises its arms high in the air and everyone says, "So-o-o big!" Can you remember playing that game?

One day when God's helper Moses was taking care of some sheep on Mount Horeb, he found that God and His love are *(raise your arms)* so-o-o big. He found out when he was *(say the following lines in rap style and ask the children to repeat each phrase after you):*

Talkin' to the Lord in the burnin' bush,
Talkin' to the Lord in the burnin' bush,
Talkin' to the Lord in the burnin' bush,
Talkin' to the Lord one day.

God was asking Moses to do a job that Moses thought was *(raise arms)* to-o-o big for him to handle. Sometimes things happen to us that seem *(raise arms)* to-o-o big for us to handle. Maybe our grandma dies, or someone in our family gets cancer, or we have to move away from our friends because Dad gets a new job. We just don't think we can handle it. But I want you to know what Moses found out when He was *(repeat verse, with children saying each line after you).*

Moses found out that God and His love are (raise arms) so-o-o big, that God can help us with every single problem. God can help, even in the times when you don't know what to do because it seems *(raise arms)* so-o-o hard. Like when you have to tell your Mom or Dad you were the one who broke the *(let children fill in "window.")* Or you have to tell a friend you didn't like the way she acted. Or you don't know what to say when you have to visit Grandma, and she is really sick. In times like that, remember what Moses found out when he was *(repeat verse, with children repeating each line after you).*

Moses found out that God and His love are *(raise arms)* so-o-o big, that God will forgive us for every sin. Even when we sin BIG, like disobeying our parents, or taking something that isn't ours, or fighting with our sister, or hurting our friend. If you think God won't love you anymore and won't give you another chance, remember God and His love are *(raise arms)* so-o-o big that He sent His Son Jesus to die in your place, to take away your sin. God raised Jesus on Easter to show us that He has power over sin and death. God's love for you is *(raise arms)* so-o-o big, you can never do anything so big or bad that God will stop loving you.

So when you have problems that are *(raise arms)* so-o-o big, remember that God and His love are *(raise arms)* so-o-o much bigger. Talk to God about them today. You don't have to wait for a burning bush! *Distribute bookmarks or books as children leave.*

Use Your Hands for Good

Truth to Teach: Jesus helps us be His servant and use our hands for good.

Scripture: Matthew 10:38–42

Preparation: You will need a wooden or cardboard cross. Trace your hand three times to make paper hands that can be attached to the cross with tape or Velcro. On one hand write "push"; on another, "steal"; and on the third, "break."

Will you play a game with me, boys and girls? It's called "Jesus Says." Do what I say **only** if I use the words "Jesus says." Let's stand to play the game.

Jesus says, use your hands for good. Pat a friend. Your friend might have a sore muscle today. *Give children time to respond.* Jesus says, use your hands for good. Hug a friend. Your friend might be lonely or sad today.

Hit a friend. *(Some children will playfully hit a friend; others won't.)* Jesus would never tell us to do that, would He? But we don't always use our hands for good. Our hands might hit or push a friend because we get angry. *Ask a child to hold the cross and tape the word "push" to it.* Or we might use our hands to break someone's toy on purpose. *Tape "break" to the cross.* Or we might want something so badly, that we take it with our hands, even though it doesn't really belong to us. *Tape "steal" to the cross.*

When we sin with our hands, we hurt others. Our sins threaten to push us away from God. But Jesus used His hands for good. He picked up a cross *(pick up cross)* with our sins on it. Soldiers put nails in His hands, and He died to take our sins away, so God could forgive us. *Take the paper sins off the cross.* That's good news! Let's give Jesus a hand. *Lead the children in applause.*

Jesus asks us to carry His cross by helping others and sharing His love. Jesus helps us to use our hands for good. Jesus says, when you see someone who is hungry, feed him. When you see someone who is sad, hug him. When you see someone who needs a friend, lend a hand. The best part is, Jesus says that when we help a friend, we are really helping Him!

Boys and girls, let's be like Jesus. Let's pick up other peoples' troubles and give them a helping hand. On your way back to your seat, use your hands to love others. Give people hugs and handshakes. *Go into the congregation with the children, giving hugs and handshakes.*

The Best Book

Truth to Teach: God gave us His Word to tell us who His Son is.

Scripture: Matthew 16:13–20

Preparation: Place a math book, reading book, and a Bible in a book bag. Buy or make a Bible bookmark for each child. Your congregation may wish to give the gift of a Bible to children of a certain age, those entering second grade, perhaps. If so, make a presentation of the Bibles to children and their parents a part of the talk. See the Bible Presentation outline on page 63.

Boys and girls, this morning I'd like to talk to you about books, especially the best book. *Take the reading book out of the book bag.* This is an important book. It's my reading book. It helped me learn to *(let children respond—read).* Now that's important! *Take out math book.* This is an important book too. It's a number book. Some people call it an arithmetic book or a math book. What can this book help us do? *Let children respond—count, add, subtract.* Now that's important!

Take Bible out of bag. Here is a very important book. In fact, it's so important, that the devil wants us to keep it closed. He doesn't want us to find out what is inside. What do you think could be so important? *Let children respond.* That's right. This book tells us about Jesus. *Turn to Matthew 16:15–16.* One day Jesus asked His disciples who they thought He was. Peter answered, "You are the Christ, the Son of the living God." No wonder this book is so important—it tells us who Jesus is. That's why I call it the best book. Here is what God's Word teaches us. Repeat the words and actions after me.

Jesus is God's Son. *(Make a cross with your fingers.)*
Who loved me so much, *(Hug self.)*
That He died on the cross to take away my sin. *(Extend arms out at sides and droop head.)*
Three days later, *(Hold up three fingers.)*
He rose from the dead. *(Lift hands high and stretch and wiggle fingers.)*
And those who believe in Jesus, *(Put hand over your heart.)*
Will have eternal life in heaven. *(Point up.)*

Now that's really, really important! I bet you'll want to read this best book every day—or have your mom or dad read it to you. Read your Bible or a Bible storybook at home today. Use this bookmark to mark your place. *If you are giving Bibles to children, invite the parents forward to be a part of the presentation. Hand out bookmarks as children leave.*

A Gift for a King

Truth to Teach: Jesus shared His love by giving His life for us; He helps us share His love with others.

Scripture: Matthew 25:34–40

Preparation: Choose a community charity or foreign mission to which the children in your congregation can contribute needed items. Place sample items—new underwear, socks, school supplies, toothpaste, toothbrush, soap, comb, food items, toys, books—in a beautifully gift-wrapped box. Duplicate a "wish list" of items children can collect. Attach lists to lunch or grocery bags. You will give each child a bag in which to collect the items and bring them to church in the following weeks.

Good morning, boys and girls. Today we want to talk about Christ our King. Jesus is our King, the ruler of our world and our hearts. Today I was thinking, what present could I buy a king? In fact, what present would I buy King Jesus? I thought and thought, and then it came to me. *Hold up gift-wrapped box and open it.* I would give Him *(take out each item and let the children name it)* underwear, socks, pencils, etc.

I know what you are thinking. These are ordinary things. Things we use every day. These aren't gifts to give to a king, especially the most special king of all, King Jesus.

But, you know what? Jesus loves these gifts! He tells us that whenever we share His love by helping people, we are really giving Him a gift. A lot of children in our world don't have the things in my box. By giving them the things they need, you will be helping Jesus too.

Show bag with wish list. Take this bag home. It has a list of things you can bring to church to share with others. Read it and pray about it with your family. Fill the bag with some things that people need. Add a card or picture or book that tells people about Jesus. *Tell children when to bring their donations and where to place them. You may want to make the gift box used in today's message large enough to be your collection box.*

We have the best King in the world. Jesus gave His life for us on the cross and rose again on Easter so our sins could be forgiven. Through Him, we will live forever in heaven. So let's give Jesus a great gift. Share with people who need to know His love. *Distribute bags as children leave.*

Don't Keep God's Love in a Box

Truth to Teach: Jesus gives us the help we need to follow His command to share His love.

Scripture: Matthew 28:18–20

Preparation: Fill a large appliance box with helium-filled red balloons. You may wish to use heart-shaped balloons if available. Gift wrap box. Use a marking pen to write "Jesus loves you" on an uninflated balloon for each child.

Point to box. Boys and girls, God has given us the gift of His love. Before Jesus went back to heaven, He asked us to share God's love with all people. What a big job! Who will help me share God's love?

Choose a volunteer and open box. (Volunteer's name), God loves you so much He sent Jesus to die on the cross in your place, to take the punishment for your sin. *Take out a balloon and hand it to the volunteer.* Now God forgives and forgives you. But He didn't stop there. God loves you so-o-o-o-o much, He sends angels to protect you from all harm and danger. *Give volunteer another balloon.*

And there is more. God loves you so much, He gives you everything you need—family, food, home, clothing. *Give the volunteer another balloon.* And still more—God gave you faith, through your Baptism, to believe all this, and He has a home ready for you in heaven when you die. *Give volunteer another balloon.*

Look at the volunteer. Now that's a lot of love. *Point to box.* God doesn't want to keep His love in a box. No way! *Ask volunteer,* Would you be willing to share God's love with the people out there in the congregation? *(Offer to help the child distribute balloons if he/she is hesitant.)* Okay, go out in the congregation and share God's love.

To the children, Look, there goes some of God's love, and some more, and more. *When the balloons are distributed, ask the volunteer to come back. (Volunteer's name),* you did a great job. Let's give our helper a round of applause.

(Point to congregation) But look, there are still a lot of people who need God's love. *Look in box.* And there is still lots of God's love left. *To volunteer,* By yourself, this job would take a long time. *To children,* Does anyone know how we can get this job done a little faster? *Let children respond.*

You mean we should all work together to share God's love? I see. By ourselves we can do a little, but together, God helps us do a lot. Let's try. Go and give a balloon to someone who needs God's love, then come back here. *Give each child a balloon to take to someone in the congregation. You may want to have adults ready to help distribute balloons.*

As the children return, Look! You were right. Everyone who has a balloon, hold up God's love! By ourselves, we can do little, but together, God helps us do a lot.

Boys and girls, sharing God's love is a big job and an important one. Don't keep God's love in a box. Ask Him to help you share it with everyone. Today I will give you a balloon with a special message on it. Blow it up and share it with a friend who needs God's love. You have a job! God will help you do it.

A Friend for Life Who Builds Us Up

Truth to Teach: Jesus is our friend for life, who helps us in all we do.

Scripture: Matthew 28:20b

Preparation: Number seven boxes of the same size, as shown. Cut holes in the three boxes that form the cross-piece so that a plastic pipe or wooden pole can be inserted through them. Place Jesus stickers for the children to take home in box 7.

Boys and girls, did you know that we have a friend for life, who helps us in everything we do? Let me show you what I mean.

Have any of you ever built something with blocks or Legos? What else do you use to build things? *Let children respond.*

Choose a young child who is likely to have difficulty making the cross on his own, but who can recognize the numerals 1–7 and follow simple directions. Today, I'd like to invite *(child's name)* to use these boxes and this plastic pipe to build a cross. Go ahead. We'll watch you build it. *Let the child work alone a few seconds.* Would you like some help? *If the child says yes, continue with directions. If the child says no, say, "I'd really like to help you. We'd make a great team." Work together to make the cross.*

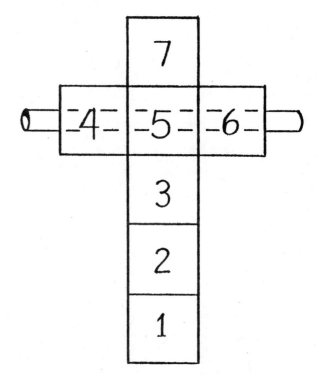

First, put box 2 on top of box 1. Good job! Now put box 3 on top of box 2. Now put boxes 4, 5, and 6 in a straight line on the floor, and put the pipe through them. *Help the child do this.* Now, let's lift these boxes and put box 5 on top of box 3. Now all we have to do is put box 7 on top. *Help as necessary.*

What a great builder! Let's give *(child's name)* a hand. It's always easier to do our work with a little help from a friend. Jesus is that kind of friend. He knew we were in deep trouble because of our sin. He knew sin separates us from God our Father. Jesus knew we needed His help, so He died on a cross *(point to cross),* built by sinful people like you and me, to pay for our sin. Because we believe that Jesus died and rose for us, our sins are forgiven and we will get to live in heaven with Jesus.

But Jesus didn't stop there. *Open box 7 and take out stickers.* Jesus didn't stop helping us after Easter. No way! Before He went to heaven to get our rooms ready, Jesus told us that He is always with us.

Jesus is our best friend who helps us at all times. He helps us when we are afraid. Raise your hand if you have ever felt afraid. *Ask several children what made them afraid. Respond to each one, "Jesus was with you," and give the child a sticker.* Raise your hand if you go to school. *Ask several children where they go to school. Respond to each one, "Jesus helps you every day at school," and give child a sticker.* Raise your hand if you know someone who doesn't believe in Jesus. *Ask several children what their own names are. Respond to each one, "(name of child), will you tell your friend about Jesus? He will be right there to help you." Give child a sticker.*

Boys and girls, Jesus is our friend for life, who is always with us to help us in all we do. Put your sticker in a place that will remind you, Jesus is always with you. *Be sure each child has a sticker.*

The Fight Inside

Truth to Teach: God sends His angels to guard us, so the evil foe can have no power over us.

Scripture: Mark 1:12–15

Preparation: You will need a white hat and a red hat. Duplicate a card with Luther's Morning Prayer (page 59) for each child.

Boys and girls, my mother taught me this prayer when I was a child. *Read Luther's Morning Prayer (page 59).*

Have you ever felt like there was a fight going on inside of you? A fight for doing what was right *(put white hat on)* against doing what was wrong *(take white hat off, put red hat on)?* That's what my mom taught me to pray about. She helped me pray that the wicked foe—the devil—would have no power over me. The fight we feel going on inside of us sometimes is the fight against temptation. Temptation is the way the devil invites us to do something we shouldn't.

Choose a boy volunteer. Let's pretend your sister just told on you. You are in deep trouble because you broke a lamp, and you told your mom you didn't. Your mom has just grounded you for two weeks, with no TV, all because your sister opened her big mouth. Your sister comes into the room *(choose a girl volunteer),* and the fight of temptation begins.

Put on the red hat and stand to the boy's left. Go ahead, tell her she's as good as gone, push her, and hope she starts a fight. Then you can fight back. She deserves it. *Put on white hat and stand to boy's right.* Now, you know it's your fault. You did something wrong. Go tell her it's okay. She was right to tell the truth.

Put on red hat and stand to left. Go ahead and call her a twit-face and hit her hard. *Put on white hat and stand to right.* No, love her and thank her for telling the truth. *Put on red hat and stand at left.* Thank her? No way! Kick her. Scream at her.

Boys and girls, who do you think is winning? Will *(boy's name)* do right or wrong? *Let children respond.* In times when we are tempted to sin, we can say the prayer my mom taught me. "Let Thy holy angels *(put on white hat)* be with me, that the wicked foe *(put on red hat)* may have no power over me."

When the devil tempted Jesus to sin, Jesus stood firm and defeated Him. Jesus defeated the devil for good when He died for our sins on the cross, and rose again from the grave. Jesus has won your fight, and He gives you the power to stand up to the devil. *Put on the white hat.* When the devil tempts you to sin, remember that Jesus sends his holy angels to keep you strong, and keep the devil from winning. Believe me, with Jesus, the devil is a real loser.

May God's holy angels be with you, that the wicked foe may have no power over you. That's my prayer for you. Keep a copy of Luther's Morning Prayer by your bed. Ask your mom or dad to teach it to you. *Hand out Luther's Morning Prayer as the children leave.*

Giving

Truth to Teach: The love Jesus showers on us motivates us to give, in return, to others and to Him.

Scripture: Mark 12:41–44

Preparation: You will need 11 pieces of candy and a miniroll of Life Savers for each child.

Good morning, boys and girls. Today I want to talk to you about giving. Another word for giving is sharing. Sometimes sharing is hard. I'll show you what I mean.

I need two helpers who like candy. *Choose two helpers and have them stand and face the congregation.* Helper Number 1, I am going to give you 10 pieces of candy. Boys and girls, let's count them together. *Have the children count from one to 10 with you as you give the child the candy.* Helper Number 2, I'm going to give you one piece of candy. Boys and girls, let's count it together. One. *Give candy to child.*

Helper Number 1, I'd like to give you a chance to share. It is your choice, but I'd like you to give one piece of candy to someone sitting in front of you. *Let child respond.* That was very kind of you. Helper Number 2, I'd like to give you a chance to share. Would you like to give one piece of candy to someone sitting in front of you? *Let child respond.*

Boys and girls, who probably had a harder time sharing? We can tell by counting what's left over. *Count the candy that Child 1 still has; do the same for Child 2. Let the children explain what happened.* That's right. Helper 1 still has nine pieces of candy. But Helper 2 gave all she had. *Collect all the candy.* Let's give our helpers a hand. They are both good sharers.

Can you think of someone who gave up everything for you and me? *Let children respond.* That's right. Jesus gave His whole life to us, by living a perfect life in our place, and then dying to take the punishment for our sin and rising again. Can anyone tell me why Jesus did that? That's right. Because He loves us so-o-o-o much. Do you think it was easy? No. But Jesus was willing to do it out of His great love for us and for His Father.

I'd like to share some Life Savers with you today. Please share some with your family and friends today. Let them remind you of God's great love for you, and how He saved your life in Jesus. *Distribute Life Savers as children leave.*

Sick

Truth to Teach: Jesus cures our sickness of sin through the forgiveness He won for us in His death on the cross.

Scripture: Luke 5:31

Preparation: You will need a doll, toy animal, or action figure (check what is currently popular with children); a "house" for the toy (could be made from a box); and objects that a child would use to play with and care for that toy. Duplicate the text of Luke 5:31 on a card for each child.

Today I want to tell you about a certain kind of sickness. You'll recognize this sickness when I tell you a story. It's a true story about a little girl I know.

This little girl loved to play with her little ponies. *Show pony.* She carefully combed the ponies' manes and tails and dressed them in different outfits. She would set them carefully in *(show house)* their special little house. You could tell this little girl loved her little pony set by the way she played with it and took care of it. Each time she finished playing, she carefully put the ponies and all of their things into their house, so nothing would get lost or broken.

One day a neighbor boy came to visit as the little girl was playing with her ponies. They were all dressed up and carefully arranged around their house. The boy happened to have a disability that made it difficult for him to walk. As he was talking to the little girl's mother, he lost his balance, and one of his feet landed right on the little ponies' house, causing the roof to cave in!

He didn't mean it. It was an accident. You could tell he felt sick about it by the look on his face. The little girl began to cry. She felt sick too. Her favorite toy was broken.

Boys and girls, have you ever felt that way because of a mistake you made, by accident or on purpose? Maybe you hit your friend, or told your mom or dad you hated them? Maybe you broke a special glass or vase or toy?

That sick feeling is caused by sin. If you have ever felt that sickness, raise your hand. Well, I've got fantastic news. There's a cure for the sickness of sin. Let me tell you the rest of the story.

The little girl, tears pouring down her face, looked up at the boy and said, "It's okay. I bet my dad can fix it." You could tell that boy was cured. The sick look disappeared, and he smiled.

The cure for the sickness of sin is forgiveness. Jesus gave us that cure by taking our sins to the cross and dying in our place. He rose on the third day, proving His power over sin, death, and the devil.

Boys and girls, we don't need to live in the sickness of sin. Because of Jesus, we have the cure—forgiveness. *Read and explain Luke 5:31 to the children.* As you go to your seats, take this card with you. Learn it with your family today, and thank Jesus for His cure for sin. *Distribute cards as children leave.*

Jesus Is Who?

Truth to Teach: Jesus is God's Son who loves us, cares for us, died and rose for us.

Scripture: Luke 9:18–20

Preparation: Gather three pictures of Jesus: Jesus with children, Jesus praying, Jesus the Good Shepherd. Write or tape the letter G on the back of the first picture, the letter O on the second, and the letter D on the third. Provide a bookmark, sticker, or picture of Jesus as a handout for each child.

As the children come forward, ask three children to stand and hold the pictures so the rest of the children can see them. Boys and girls, I'm excited to see you here today. I can tell that you love Jesus and are happy to come to worship Him. Look at these pictures. *Point to each picture.* Who is in picture number 1? picture number 2? picture number 3?

Think about this, who is Jesus? *Point to pictures.* In the first picture, Jesus looks like a big brother or a friend, taking care of children. Is that what Jesus is, a brother?

In the second picture, Jesus is praying, like we do. Is Jesus like a pastor or a priest, who teaches us to pray and helps us pray? In the third picture, Jesus is a shepherd. Is that what Jesus is, a shepherd who takes care of little lambs?

Boys and girls, Jesus is all that and more! If we turn each picture around *(help children turn pictures),* we find that Jesus is G-O-D. God!

Jesus is our strong and powerful God, *(turn G back to picture 1)* sent by His Father to love us and give His life for us on the cross. *Turn O back to picture 2.* Jesus is like our pastor, praying for us and teaching us to pray. *Turn D back to picture 3.* Jesus is our Shepherd, caring for us and protecting us from danger.

With a God like this, should we keep our love for Jesus a secret? *Let children respond.* So when someone says, "Who loved you enough to die for you," you'll say—*(let children respond)* Jesus! When you need help, you'll go to—Jesus! When people say, "Why do you go to church," "Why do you pray at the lunch table," "Why are you kind to people who are mean to you," you will say, because I love—Jesus!

Boys and girls, you are the greatest! Your love for Jesus shows.

Take a picture of Jesus with you and share it with a friend. *Distribute pictures as children leave.*

Extravagant

Truth to Teach: God's love in Jesus is extravagant!

Scripture: Luke 15:1–3, 11–32

Preparation: Gather a large bowl, ice cream scoop, ice cream and whipped cream (can be kept in a cooler), chocolate sauce and toppings, nuts, cherries, M&M's, sprinkles, and an apron.

Boys and girls, God's love is EXTRAVAGANT. That's a big word, say it after me—EX-TRA-VA-GANT. But what does it mean? Let me show you.

Put on apron. When I was growing up, we didn't get to eat ice cream very much, and when we did, it was a special treat. I always dreamed of having an EXTRAVAGANT ice cream treat. *Ask a helper to hold the bowl. Continue to talk as you scoop ice cream into bowl.*

For me, an *(motion for children to speak with you)* EXTRAVAGANT ice cream treat wasn't just one scoop *(put one scoop in bowl),* or two scoops *(continue adding scoops),* or three scoops. It was four scoops. Now that's *(lead the children in speaking with you)* EXTRAVAGANT!

But wait a minute. EXTRAVAGANT is more. It's putting on as much chocolate sauce as you want. You see, my mom was an expert at keeping the chocolate to a very small amount. She kept the chocolate sauce in the refrigerator and put a very tiny hole in the can. Have you ever tried to get thick, cold chocolate out of a tiny hole in the chocolate sauce can? *Pour a generous amount of chocolate over the ice cream.* Now that's—EXTRAVAGANT.

But EXTRAVAGANT is even more. We need to add nuts. *Sprinkle nuts.* Now that's— EXTRAVAGANT. Then we need some M&M's. *Continue to add items, helping the children repeat "Now that's EXTRAVAGANT" with you.* We need lots of whipped cream. And sprinkles.

Now you're probably thinking, I thought we were going to talk about God's love. What's all this about ice cream? I'll tell you. There is something even more EXTRAVAGANT than this ice cream sundae. What is it? *Let children respond.*

That's right. God's love is so *(lead children in saying EXTRAVAGANT)* that He sent His only Son Jesus to give His life on the cross for us and take the punishment for our sins. Jesus didn't just give us a hand or a foot or a mouth. He gave His whole self for us. Giving up one's life for another, now that's *(EXTRAVAGANT)* love.

When you eat ice cream this week, remember to thank God for His *(EXTRAVAGANT)* love. *You may want to give each child a clean plastic spoon and let them take a bite of ice cream as they leave.*

Rejoice

Truth to Teach: God rejoices when sinners repent.

Scripture: Luke 15:7

Preparation: You will need two handbells that ring in harmony. (Or have a keyboard player ready to play two notes of a chord.) Make a "Rejoice Stick" for each child. Use a marking pen to write the word "Rejoice" on a craft stick. Slip short pieces of yarn through jingle bells and tape the yarn to the sticks. If very young toddlers come forward for the message, give their sticks to their parents so they can help the children use them safely.

Here we are in God's house again, where He pours out His love on us in the waters of Baptism, serves us His love through Holy Communion, and tells us in His Word of His loving plan to save us through the death of His Son. Isn't it great to be here in His house, to receive *(stretch out your arms)* God's hug of love?

Just think. God does all of this for us because He loves us. If you agree, say "Rejoice." God's love is so strong *(show your muscles),* that He will never stop loving us. If you agree, say "Rejoice."

God loves us so much, He helps us love Him back. I wonder what we could do that would make God, not just happy *(ring one bell),* or glad *(ring second bell),* but would make Him rejoice *(ring both bells).* "Rejoice" means being happy *(ring one bell)* and glad *(ring second bell)* at the same time. Rejoice means being filled with joy and happiness and gladness to the very top *(stand),* to overflowing. Let me show you what I mean.

Obeying Mom and Dad makes God happy *(ring one bell).* Can anyone tell me about a time you obeyed Mom and Dad? *Ring one bell for every answer.* Doing your best makes God glad *(ring one bell).* Can anyone tell about doing your best at school or sports or day care this week? *Ring one bell for each answer.*

But what makes God rejoice? Our Bible verse tells us God rejoices when we say we are sorry for our sin and ask Him to forgive us. Maybe we sin against a person big time, we hurt our friend, or call our sister a name, or we're just plain mean. Maybe we take a friend's toy and break it in anger.

But then God's Holy Spirit helps us think of God's great love. We tell the person we are sorry, and ask for forgiveness. We tell God we are sorry and ask for His forgiveness. That's when God rejoices *(ring both bells and stand)!* He is happy and glad and filled to the top with overflowing joy. Can anyone remember saying "I'm sorry" and asking for forgiveness this week? *Ring both bells for each response.*

God rejoices each time we repent and tell Him we are sorry for our sins. He gladly forgives us for the sake of Jesus, who gave His life so our sins could be forgiven. Boys and girls, let's keep God rejoicing all week. Let's tell the people we sin against, and God, that we are sorry. Take a Rejoice Stick with you. Every time you hear someone at home say, "I'm sorry," ring your Rejoice Stick. *Distribute sticks as children leave. Let parents carry the sticks for very young toddlers.*

Two Masters

Truth to Teach: God strengthens us through His Holy Spirit to serve Him only.

Scripture: Luke 16:1–13

Preparation: Prepare an adult helper, as indicated, and practice together ahead of time. You will need two aprons, a small table or TV tray, a chair, a bowl of candy, five plastic bags, construction paper, scissors, a card with a dollar sign, and a card with the word "God."

Boys and girls, this is my friend, *(name of adult helper)*. We need a volunteer this morning. *Choose an older child.* Let's put this apron on you and get started. Sit behind this table. We only have a few minutes to work. *Stand to the child's right, with your helper to the child's left.* I have five teens coming to talk to me and I want to give each of them an equal amount of candy from my bowl. Please put two of each kind in the five plastic bags. But there is only one red gumball for each one.

Adult Helper: *Give construction paper and scissors to child.* I need some paper hearts cut out for my party. Please do that first. You may begin.

Leader: Now wait a minute. The teens are coming any minute. Put the candy in the bags first.

Adult Helper: I really need those hearts. Please cut my hearts first.

Leader: No! Put the candy in the bags.

Adult Helper: Cut the shapes!

Leader: Times up. Boys and girls, why couldn't *(child's name)* get the work done? That's right. You can't have two people telling you what to do. You can only listen to and follow one person at a time. That's what God says in His Word, "A man can't have two masters."

Let me show you what God means. *Invite a second child to stand. Tie on apron.* The world says money is important. *Tape dollar sign to second child's apron.* Make lots of it. Cheat, steal if you have to. But God says, "Put Me first." *Tape "God" to first child's apron and have the children stand side-by-side.* God loves you so much, He sent His Son Jesus to die for you and pay for your sins. In your Baptism, He gives you the faith to follow Him and the strength to put Him first.

God says, "Put Me first. Worship Me every Sunday. Read My Word. Pray every day." Who will you follow, *(point to children)* the world's way, or God's way? Go back to your seats and tell your family whom you listen to and follow.

God's Persistent Love

Truth to Teach: God never gives up on His people. His love never stops.

Scripture: Luke 20:9–19; Jeremiah 31:3

Preparation: You will need a jump rope.

Boys and girls, today I'd like to talk to you about Jesus and His persistent love. Say that big word after me—per-r-rsistent. That's a big word that describes, or tells us about, God's love. Believe it or not, many of you have already been per-r-rsistent. Let me show you. I need a volunteer who can jump rope. *Choose volunteer.*

(Child's name), do you like to jump rope? Go ahead and show us your stuff. *Be sure the other children are out of the rope's way and let the child jump.* Let's give *(child's name)* a round of applause. That was great. *(Child's name),* how long did it take you to learn to jump rope? What would have happened if you would have given up after you missed a few times? You would have missed all the fun of jumping rope. But you were per-r-rsistent. You didn't give up, and now you enjoy the fun of jumping rope. Thank you.

Now I need a volunteer who knows how to whistle. *Choose a volunteer. (Child's name),* show us how you can whistle. Maybe you could whistle "Jesus Loves Me." *Let child whistle.* Good job. Let's give *(child's name)* a hand. *(Child's name),* could you always whistle? How long did it take you to learn? What would have happened if you would have given up? Because you were per-r-rsistent, you have the joy of whistling.

Boys and girls, God is per-r-rsistent in His love for us. When we sin, does God say, "I give up. I'm not going to love you anymore"? Of course not. God says, "I love you so much, I let my only Son die to take the punishment for your sin. I want you to live in heaven with Me. I forgive you and will help you to live in My love."

God's love is per-r-rsistent. When we do something wrong and tell God we are sorry, He is *(lead children in saying "per-r-rsistent").* When it is dark and we are afraid, God is—per-r-rsistent in taking care of us. When we are hungry, God is—per-r-rsistent in feeding us. God loves us so much that He sticks with us, no matter what! Our God is—per-r-rsistent. What a great God we have!

The Promise of Life

Truth to Teach: Jesus won everlasting life for us through His perfect life, death, and resurrection.

Scripture: John 3:16

Preparation: Fill a large jar with wrapped candy. You will need a Bible.

Show jar of candy. This jar of candy will help us remember an important promise from God—His sweet promise of everlasting life.

I want to make a promise to you. I promise to give each of you a piece of candy today. How many of you believe me? You know what? You are absolutely right to believe me!

Take a piece of candy from the jar, unwrap it slowly, and enjoy eating it. This candy is really good—but what will finally happen to it? That's right. Whether I take my time and eat it slowly, or chew it up real fast, sooner or later the candy will be gone. Wouldn't it be great to have a piece of candy that would never go away? A lot of the things we are promised don't last, do they? A vacation trip, a new bike, a party—sooner or later, the promised stuff is over, worn out, gone.

Boys and girls, I know a promise that will last forever. It is the promise of everlasting life with Jesus in heaven. Listen to what Jesus says in John 3:16. *Read passage from Bible.* Because God's Holy Spirit gave you faith and helps you believe that Jesus died in your place and rose again on Easter morning, you will live forever in heaven.

Jesus' promise is very different than mine. I can only promise a piece of candy that will be used up. But Jesus' promise of life with Him in heaven will last forever. Believe me, you can count on Jesus to keep His promises. As you go back, take a piece of candy. Eat it at home. Let it remind you that the best and sweetest promise of all is the promise of everlasting life in heaven that Jesus won for us. *Distribute candy.*

Heavenly Food That Is Just Out of This World

Truth to Teach: God will keep your faith strong in Jesus, the Bread of Life.

Scripture: John 6:35

Preparation: Prepare a plate of food, perhaps peas, a hot dog, potato chips, and cookies. You will need a second plate with a Bible and a cross or picture of Jesus. Draw a slice of bread on a piece of paper. Write the text of John 6:35 on it. Duplicate on cardstock for each child.

Boys and girls, today God wants you to know that He gives you something very special to keep your love for Jesus strong. God's Word calls that special thing the "Bread of Life." To help you understand, I've brought two plates of food. Who can tell me what is on the first one? *Let children identify the food items.*

Raise your hand if your mom or dad has ever said to you, "You have to clean your plate before you can leave the table." Why do moms and dads do that? Is it because they want to make our lives miserable? *Let children respond; then point to vegetables on plate.* Raise your hand if your mom or dad has ever said to you, "Make sure to eat all of your vegetables." Why do moms and dads do that? Is it because they don't like you? *Let children respond.*

Moms and dads know something important. We need to eat the right kinds of food—including vegetables—to help our bodies grow big and strong. Without the right foods, what would happen to our bodies? *Let children respond.*

Our bodies are a gift from God, and He helps us keep them strong and healthy. But even more important—our love for Jesus needs to be strong and healthy. We can't keep it strong by ourselves. God the Father gave us something very special to help us. *Show second plate with a Bible and a cross.* Who can tell us what is on this plate? That's right, a cross and a Bible. *Hold up cross.* God sent His Son Jesus from heaven to do what no one else could do. Jesus saved us from hell by dying on the cross in our place, and rising again on Easter. Those who believe in Him will live forever with Him in heaven. We love Jesus for doing that, right?

God gives us His Word to keep our faith and love for Jesus strong and healthy. As we read and learn about Jesus, the Bread of Life *(put cross in Bible),* God sends His Holy Spirit to keep our faith and love strong.

That's why your parents say, "It's time for devotions," or "It's Sunday, time to go to church." They know a good helping of Jesus, the Bread of Life, every day will keep your love for Him from fading away. Isn't it wonderful that our great God gives us what we need to keep our bodies strong, and gives us what we need to keep our love for Jesus strong? As you go back, pick up a piece of the Bread of Life and memorize it this week. *Distribute bread cards as the children leave.*

All Tied Up

Truth to Teach: Jesus frees us from sin.

Scripture: John 8:31–36

Preparation: Tear strips of cloth that can be used to gently tie a child's hands, feet, and mouth. Prepare a child beforehand, or choose a child who is very comfortable with you.

Boys and girls, today we want to talk about the truth of sin.

Choose a volunteer, or ask the child you have prepared to help you. The truth is, at times, we use our hands to sin. We might hit the person in front of us, or take a cookie after Mom said no. Let's tie these hands together to remind us of the sins we do with our hands. *Securely tie child's hands with strip of cloth in such a way that the child will not be unable to untie it alone.*

The truth is, our feet can get us into trouble when we use them to sin. We might kick the dog, or our sister. We might walk out of the house, right past the dishes we were supposed to put away before we went out to play. The sins of our feet can get us into trouble. Let's tie these feet together to remind us of the sins we do with our feet. *Gently tie a cloth strip around child's ankles, being sure he/she can retain balance.*

What about our mouth? The truth is, our mouth can get us into trouble. We might yell, or say angry words, or tell a lie, or spread rumors and gossip. Let's tie a cloth around this mouth to remind us of the sins of our mouth. *Gently tie cloth over child's mouth.*

Sin makes us a prisoner of the devil, and we are bound for hell. *Speak to volunteer.* Can you get yourself out of this mess? Go ahead, free yourself from sin. *Let child struggle a moment.* There is no way you can save yourself, is there?

The truth is, Jesus frees us from sin. Jesus earned us forgiveness for sins of our mouth by dying on the cross to take our punishment. *Untie cloth around head.* Jesus sets us free to say good things about others and sing praises to Him. Jesus forgives the sins of our feet *(untie feet),* and helps us walk in His ways. Jesus forgives the sins of our hands *(untie hands),* and sets us free to serve others.

Remind children that they should never tie someone up in play, or let anyone else tie them up. Explain that you wanted them to understand how sad it is to be tied up in sin, and how wonderful it is to be free in Jesus. Go and serve the Lord. You are free, because Jesus died for you and me!

A Friend for Life Who Changes Us

Truth to Teach: God's Holy Spirit changes our spiritual blindness to healing sight as we look to Christ's love through the eyes of faith.

Scripture: John 9:39

Preparation: Prepare an older child to help you. Place a Bible and a cross in a bag. You will need a blindfold. Purchase an inexpensive Bible story book for each child. (Consider the *PassAlong Arch Book* series from Concordia Publishing House. The books begin with a PassAlong page so children can share their book, and their faith, with a friend. Among the 16 titles are *Baby Jesus, Prince of Peace,* order no. 59-1471; *Jesus and the Little Children,* order no 59-1481; and *God's Easter Plan,* order no. 59-1461.)

Boys and girls, if you believe that Jesus changes us—makes us different—raise your hand. I believe it too! Let me show you what I mean. First I need my friend who said he/she wouldn't mind being blindfolded. *Blindfold child you prepared.*

I'm going to show our friend two things. Don't slip and say the answer. *Pull Bible out of bag and hold it up in front of blindfolded child.* Okay, *(child's name),* what am I holding? You can't tell, can you? You can't see because you are blindfolded.

A lot of people who aren't Christians—who haven't been changed by God's Holy Spirit—don't know what this is either. They may even open it and look at it, but, to them, it is just another ... Don't say it. We don't want to give it away. *Ask another child to hold the Bible next to the blindfolded child.*

Hold up cross. Okay, *(child's name),* I'm holding something else up in front of you. Can you tell me what it is? Of course you can't, you're blindfolded. A lot of people who aren't Christians—who haven't been changed—have no idea what this is either. They might even wear one, or hang it on their wall, but they have no idea what happened on one like it. They think it's just a nice ... Don't say anything! We don't want to give it away. *Ask another volunteer to stand on the other side of the blindfolded child and hold the cross.*

Boys and girls, what happens to people who live their whole lives without being changed, and never learn what these things mean? What do they miss? *Children might respond, "Jesus," "life in heaven," etc.*

I have great news. God wants everyone to see and know His love and forgiveness in Jesus. He wants it so badly, He sends His Holy Spirit to help us. Through our Baptism and through our learning of God's Word, the Holy Spirit gives us faith. God *(take off blindfold)* heals the blindness of our sin and gives us the faith to see. *Point to Bible.* What is this? That's right. God helps us see and believe the truth of His Word, His message of salvation, love, and forgiveness. *Point to cross.* What is this? That's right, a cross like the one Jesus died on to pay the price for our sin. He rose again on Easter so that all who believe in Him may live with Him in heaven.

Do you know someone who can't see Jesus' love? I would like you to take a book about Jesus with you today. After you read the book with your family, share your book with a friend. Explain what the Bible is, and what a cross means. Ask God's Holy Spirit to work through you to change your friend. *Distribute books as children leave.*

Guess Who

Truth to Teach: God knows and leads His people like a loving shepherd leads his sheep.

Scripture: John 10:1–10

Preparation: Tape messages, as indicated, to play for the children. Messages 3 and 5 should be your pastor's voice. Messages 1, 2, and 4 should be three different individuals. Duplicate a Jesus, the Good Shepherd card, page 61, for each child.

I'd like to play a game with you this morning. It's called "Follow the Voice." I'll play a tape, and you listen to the voice and follow the directions. Ready? *Play message 1: Stand up and clap your hands.* Great! Are you ready for the next message? *Play message 2: Turn to a friend and shake hands.* Good! Listen to the next voice. *Play message 3 (pastor's voice): Turn around and wave to your parents.* Great! You are ready for the next voice. *Play message 4: Now, boys and girls, turn around, sit down, and listen to the rest of the children's message.* Boys and girls, you are great listeners.

Who can tell me, did you recognize pastor's *(or "my")* voice? What did he tell you to do? *Let children respond.* That's right. You know pastor's voice, and you can follow what he says. Jesus says, "My sheep hear My voice, and I know them and they follow Me." Have any of you ever heard what Jesus' voice sounds like? I haven't either. But I bet you can recognize the things Jesus tells us.

Would Jesus say, "Hurt people who hurt you"? *Let children respond to each statement.* Would Jesus say, "If someone hits you, punch their lights out"? Would Jesus say, "Forgive and love people who are mean to you"? You do know Jesus' voice! You have Christian ears! God's Holy Spirit helps you know and listen to Jesus.

I have one more message for you. *Play message 5: Jesus says, "My sheep (that's you) hear my voice. I know them and they listen and follow me."* As you go back to your seats, take a picture of Jesus, our Good Shepherd, and listen to what He says to you in church today. *Distribute pictures as children leave.*

Death—No Problem

Truth to Teach: Thanks to Jesus' redeeming work on the cross, death has no power over us.

Scripture: John 11:1–44

Preparation: You will need a potted flower and a flower bulb. Place a tulip bulb in a plastic bag for each child. Staple a card with the text of John 11:25–26a to each bag. (*Editor's Note:* This talk includes a true story about the author's brother, Robert.)

Hold up potted flower. Look at this beautiful flower. *Hold up bulb.* Who can tell me what this is? That's right. It's a tulip *(or whatever flower you brought)* bulb. Something really strange happened the other day. I heard this bulb talking to this flower. Here's what they said. *Move bulb and pot as if they were puppets.*

Bulb: I am really scared.

Flower: I'm sorry to hear that. What are you afraid of?

Bulb: I'm afraid I won't be a beautiful flower like you.

Flower: Why do you think that?

Bulb: Well, I heard that first they dig a hole. Then they put me in it and cover me up with dirt! I'm afraid I won't rise up out of the ground and become a beautiful flower.

Flower: Believe me, there is nothing to worry about! At the right time, you will come out of the ground and be a beautiful flower, just like me.

Do you think the flower and bulb really talked? You're right, they didn't. But let's keep pretending. Why was the bulb afraid? *Let children respond.* Many people are afraid, that when they die, they are going to stay dead in the ground. We don't believe that, do we!

I know a true story about a little boy named Robert, who didn't believe it either. When Robert was five years old, he became very sick with leukemia. The doctors said he would die before his sixth birthday. Each night, Robert's mom and dad would pray with him. One night Mom and Dad were so sad, thinking about Robert dying, that they began to cry. Five-year-old Robert looked at them and said, "Mom and Dad, I know you are sad because you are going to miss me. But I won't be sad. I'll be with Jesus in heaven!"

Boys and girls, Robert thought about dying and said, "Death—no problem!" He knew Jesus died and rose again so that Robert too could rise from the dead and go to live in heaven with Him.

Hold up bulb. Some day you will die. *Hold up flower.* But it won't be a problem. Because of Jesus, you will rise from the dead and live in heaven. So when it is your turn to face death, you can say, just like Robert, "Death—no problem! I'm going to live with Jesus." As you go back, take a tulip bulb to plant. Read the card with your family. It says, "I am the resurrection and the life. He who believes in Me will live, even though he dies; and whoever lives and believes in Me will never die." Together you can say, "Death—no problem!" *Distribute bulbs.*

Focused

Truth to Teach: God's Holy Spirit keeps our eyes focused on Jesus.

Scripture: John 12:20–26

Preparation: You will need to set up a filmstrip projector or overhead, ready to show a picture or transparency of Jesus. You will need some dollar bills; a bat and ball, or some other sports equipment; and a toy or computer game. Purchase an inexpensive picture of Jesus for each child.

This morning we want to talk about keeping our eyes focused on Jesus. To help us, I will show you a picture of *(turn projector or overhead on and invite children to respond with you)* Jesus.

Boys and girls, just before a Christian father died, he talked to his family as they gathered around his bed. He said, "You don't have to worry about how you'll get along without me." You see, the family was worried about how they would pay for food and clothing and a place to live. The dad said, "Just keep your eyes on Jesus. Love Him and trust Him. Even though you have to work hard, He will take care of you."

That father was a wise man. But it's not as easy as it sounds to keep your eyes focused on Jesus. Sometimes our eyes focus on other things. Like money. *Show money and begin to blur the picture of Jesus.* Or sports. *Show sports equipment and blur the picture some more.* Or just things. *Show the toy or computer game and blur the picture until it is completely out of focus.*

Now, there's nothing wrong with these things *(point to items you just displayed)*. But if we allow these things to be the focus of our lives, what might happen? That's right, we might forget about Jesus. We might forget that He died to win us forgiveness for our sins. We might forget that He came alive again on Easter so we can live for Him. Then *(turn off projector or overhead)*, our love for Jesus might disappear altogether.

To tell you the truth, boys and girls, it's impossible for us to keep our eyes focused on Jesus by ourselves. But God sends His Holy Spirit to us in many ways to help us keep our eyes on Jesus. *Turn on projector or overhead.* God invites us to come to church and worship Him. *Focus the picture a little.* He gives us time in Sunday school and vacation Bible school to learn about Him. *Focus a little more.* He gives us a family to tell us about Jesus *(focus more)* and pray with us *(focus clearly)*. Look, God keeps our eyes on Jesus. He is in sharp focus for us. As you go back to your seats, take a picture of Jesus with you. Talk with your family about how important it is to help each other keep our eyes focused on Jesus. With God's help, our eternal life depends on it! *Distribute pictures as children leave.*

Jesus' Love Never Runs Out

Truth to Teach: Jesus' love for us never runs out.

Scripture: John 15:12–13

Preparation: Cut a heart pattern from an 8½″ × 11″ piece of paper. Duplicate 50 hearts on red paper and cut them out. Stretch a long piece of red yarn out on the floor. Tape hearts to the yarn, leaving a space the width of a heart between them. Tie one end of the heart string to a cross. Lay the first heart on the cross, then layer all the other hearts on top, one at a time. Place the pile of hearts in a gift bag. Have a heart sticker or heart-shaped sucker for each child.

This morning, boys and girls, let's talk about the most precious thing in the whole world—Jesus' love. Did you know that Jesus' love never runs out?

What will happen if you keep driving and driving and driving a car? *(It will run out of gas.)* What happens if you keep eating and eating popcorn out of a bowl? *(It will be all gone.)* What will happen if you keep eating and eating a candy bar? When the last bite is gone, you run out of *(lead the children in saying "candy bar")*.

But look at what never stops *(ask a child to start pulling out hearts)*—Jesus love! *Gently stop the child.* Stop! If Jesus saw someone on the side of the road whose car had run out of gas, would He pass them by? No way! Even though that person ran out of gas, Jesus wouldn't run out of love. He would stop and help because, Jesus' love *(lead children in speaking with you)* never runs out.

Okay, start pulling again. *(After a moment)* Stop. If Jesus saw a family who was hungry because they ran out of food, would Jesus pass them by? No way! They may be out of food, but Jesus' love *(together)* never runs out.

Let's pull some more. *(After a moment)* Stop. Do you sometimes feel like you've run out of love, when your brother hits you, or your friend calls you a name, or when a grown-up disappoints you? Do you sometimes get mad, or yell, or hit someone? *Let children respond.* Does Jesus run out of love? *Signal child to start pulling again until you can take the cross out of the bag.*

No way! Jesus loved us so much that He didn't pass us by. He gave His life for us *(hold up cross)* on a cross, to pay for our sins. That's because Jesus' love *(together)* never runs out. As you go today, I want each of you to have a sucker (sticker). Your sucker will finally run out (or you might lose your sticker), but Jesus' love *(together)* never runs out. *Distribute suckers or stickers.*

The Best Gift

Truth to Teach: God's Holy Spirit gives us our faith in Jesus—the best gift of all.

Scripture: Romans 5:1–2

Preparation: You will need a toy or computer game, a poster of Walt Disney World (or a similar spot which children enjoy), a cross, and a red cloth. Place a bow on each object. You may want to have an assistant bring out each "gift" as you talk about it. Have a Baptism sticker—or other Baptism remembrance—for each child.

I need your help, boys and girls. I need to pick the best, most fantastic, incredible gift anyone could have. This gift is for a very good friend, so I want this gift to be the best. Will you help me? I'll show you three gifts, and you pick the best one for my friend.

Show toy or computer game. First is a brand new *(name of object)*. Boy, my friend would love this. *Ask a child to hold it.*

Show the poster. Next is a trip to Walt Disney World for his whole family—all expenses paid. I think my friend would really love this. *Ask a child to hold it.*

The third gift *(hold up cross)* is faith in Jesus. It includes *(tie red scarf to cross)* forgiveness of my friend's sins, and eternal life in heaven. I think my friend would like this gift too.

Now, you vote. I'll point to a gift and you raise your hand if you think it would be the best gift. *Let the children vote for each item. Count votes each time.*

Boys and girls, why did you vote the way you did? *Let children respond.* After listening to you, I believe the best gift my friend could have is the gift of faith in Jesus. The *(name of toy or game)* would be great, but after a while it would wear out, or my friend would get tired of it. The trip to Walt Disney World would be fun, but it would end, and after a while, even the good memories would be forgotten. But faith in Jesus! This gift is the way to heaven through the death of Jesus *(point to cross)* on a cross, and His resurrection from the grave. This gift of faith and eternal life will never, ever end. This is the gift I'm going to ask God's Holy Spirit to give to my friend.

Thanks for helping me decide. I have a gift for you today that will remind you of the great gift God's Holy Spirit gave you at your Baptism. Put your sticker in a place where you will see it every day. It will remind you of your greatest gift. *Distribute stickers as children leave.*

Don't Encourage

Truth to Teach: God helps us show others how Christians live.

Scripture: 1 Corinthians 8:9–13

Preparation: Fill a box with small packages of M&M's. Make two posterboard signs reading "Bad Words." Decorate with the punctuation marks and symbols used to denote expletives in cartoons.

This morning, boys and girls, I want you to remember two words—don't encourage. Say them after me. Don't encourage. I know some of you are thinking, what's he talking about? I thought we're supposed to encourage people. Let me explain what I mean by saying "don't encourage."

Show box of candy. The eighth grade students are selling candy to earn money for their class trip. Brian has been walking around the school, asking people to buy M&M's. He sets the box down and walks over to talk to a classmate. You and a friend see this big box of candy. Your friend *(demonstrate)* takes a bag of M&M's out of the box and hides it behind his back. What do you do? *Let children respond.* What will Jesus help you do? That's right. Jesus can help you be strong enough to do what's right, and even to help your friend do what's right. That's what I mean by "don't encourage." Don't encourage your friends to do what's wrong, but help them do what's right.

Jesus might help you tell your friend, "M&M's would be great, but they cost 50 cents. Do you think we have enough money to buy some?" I know what you would do next. You would take the M&M's from your friend and put them back in the box, because we *(lead the children in speaking with you)* don't encourage friends to do what is wrong. We help them to do what is right!

Think about this. Two friends are over at your house. One of your friends says a bad word. It is too bad to say in church. *Hold up sign.* The other friend laughs and says a bad word *(hold up second sign)* too. They wait for you to say the next bad word. What do you do? *Let children respond.*

I can hear what Jesus will help you do. You will say, "I don't like those words. We don't use them around here." That's because we *(lead children)* don't encourage friends to do what is wrong. We help them to do what is right!

That's not always easy. Your friends might get mad at you. Or call you a wimp. So why not just let them say bad words? What's the big deal? The big deal is, we want others to know how important Jesus is. We don't want to let them think that Jesus likes what's wrong. Jesus hates stealing and bad words and sin. But He loves us so much, that He died on the cross to take away all the wrong things we do. We want our friends to know that Jesus died and rose again to win us eternal life in heaven.

Boys and girls, let's make a promise together. Repeat the words after me. Don't encourage/what is wrong,/but help others/do what's right. Good. Take some M&M's to help you remember your promise. Jesus will help you too. *Distribute candy as children leave.*

Do I Have To?

Truth to Teach: Jesus gives us the ability to put others first and ourselves second.

Scripture: Galatians 5:13–14

Preparation: Place a candy bar for each child in a plastic bag. Staple a card with the text of Galatians 5:14b to each bag. You will need one candy bar to display.

Boys and girls, listen carefully to these words and how I say them. Tell me who sometimes sounds like this. *(Whine)* Do I have to? Say it with me. Do I have too? What is that sound? That's right. It's the sound of whining and complaining. Raise your hand if you have ever said those words. I have too.

One time there was a mom who never had enough money to buy two candy bars so her son and his friend could both have one. She would buy one candy bar *(hold up candy)* for them to share. The problem was, she wasn't very good at breaking the candy bar into two even pieces. *Unwrap candy bar. Break it unevenly.* Then the mom would put the small piece in one hand and the big piece in the other, and hold the little piece in front of her son, and the big piece in front of his friend.

The son would wait, hoping the friend would take the little piece. But he never did. He always took the big piece. The son wanted to scream, "Do I have to!"

Jesus tells us to love our neighbor as ourselves, to put our friend first and treat him or her like we would like to be treated. But that is so hard!

Let's say we're watching TV and Mom comes in and says, "I really need help with the dishes. Please come and help me." What are we tempted to say? *Lead children in saying "Do I have to?"* Or lets say we have a whole bag of candy and our brother asks for some. Mom says to share. What are we tempted to say? *(Together)* Do I have to?

By ourselves, boys and girls, it's impossible to stop saying "Do I have to?" But God doesn't want the sin of selfishness to separate us from Him. He loves us so much that He asked His Son Jesus to do much more than wash the dishes or share candy. God sent Jesus to give His life on the cross to take the punishment for our sins, so we can be forgiven. Instead of saying "Do I have to," Jesus said, "If it is Your will, I will."

Boys and girls, that same Jesus who died for you will help you love your neighbor. Take a candy bar with you and share it with a friend today. If it breaks into a big piece and a little piece, ask Jesus to help you give your friend the big one. *Distribute candy.*

Harmony

Truth to Teach: God's Holy Spirit gives us the ability to forgive and live in harmony with others.

Scripture: Ephesians 4:32

Preparation: Make a sticker or button for each child, reading: "Promote harmony. Forgive one another." If your congregation has a handbell choir, ask an adult to help children ring four bells—three that ring in harmony, and one that's discordant. If not, ask an adult to help children play notes on a keyboard. You may want to do this message in conjunction with the confession and absolution.

Boys and girls, I'm sorry to have to tell you that our world and our home and our school and our community are a mess. I want you to hear what they sound like. *Choose three volunteers. Ask the adult to give the children two bells that ring in harmony, plus the one that is discordant.*

When I point to you, ring the bells. *Some of the children may have trouble producing a sound. Help them until they are all ringing.* Boys and girls, does your house ever sound like that? It is horrible! Our world is out of tune, and do you know what makes it out of tune? Sin *(point and let the children ring bells).* Sin *(point)* hurts me. Sin *(point)* makes others hurt. Sin *(point)* makes the whole family hurt. Sin *(point)* makes classrooms hurt. Sin *(point)* makes friends hurt. Sin *(point)* makes the church hurt. Let's face it, sin *(point)* is a real pain!

Sometimes we don't follow directions *(point).* Sometimes we talk when we're supposed to be quiet *(point).* And sometimes, we're downright mean to each other *(point).* That's when God helps us to remember the price Jesus paid for our sin on the cross. God helps us feel sorry for our sins and confess them.

I think we need a time of confession. I'll say a sin and, as God helps you, say together, "I'm sorry." *You may ask the congregation to join with you.*

For the sin of disobeying *(point),* God's people say, *(lead the children and congregation)* I'm sorry. For the sin of being rude to my neighbor *(point),* God's people say, I'm sorry. For the sin of talking when asked to be quiet *(point),* God's people say, "I'm sorry."

Now, let's find that out-of-tune bell. *The assistant may help the children ring two bells at a time until they discover the one that is discordant. Replace that bell with a bell that will produce a harmonious sound. Ask the children to ring the bells.*

Now that sounds better. *(Point)* It is the sound of forgiveness. *Ask your pastor to speak the words of absolution (or you pronounce them) as you point.* By the blood of Jesus, you are forgiven *(point),* in the name of the Father *(point)* and of the Son *(point)* and of the Holy Spirit *(point).* Amen.

Ask God to be with you today and give you the power to use His gift of forgiveness to help our world stay in harmony *(point)*—in tune, wherever we go. Wear a sticker today to help you remember: Promote harmony. Forgive one another. *Distribute stickers as children leave.*

Miss Lulu

Truth to Teach: God gives us the power to imitate Christ's love, so others can see His love through us.

Scripture: Ephesians 5:1–2

Preparation: You will need a candy bar for demonstration, a candy bar for each child, and a Bible.

Boys and girls, when I was a little boy, a lot of times my mom would say to me, "Remember, be a good Christian example in everything you do and say today." What do you think my mom meant? *Let children respond.* Yes, she meant, "Whatever you say or do, let Jesus' love shine through."

One time an older lady named Miss Lulu asked me to rake her leaves. It was a big yard, but Mom said I should do it for free. When I was all finished, Miss Lulu offered to pay me. I told her no, I wouldn't take money. Miss Lulu told me to wait. She went into the house, and came back with my favorite *(show it)* candy bar. Well, Mom hadn't said that I couldn't have candy, and I had worked really hard, so I said thank you and took it.

I got on my bike and rode to the park. I had just sat down in my favorite resting spot, and taken the candy out of my pocket, when two friends rode up. Oh, no! I had worked so hard for this *(show candy)* and it was my favorite! But I remembered my mom's words, "Be a good Christian example today, *(your name)*." So what do you think I did? That's right. I broke the candy bar into three pieces and shared it. *(Break the candy bar into three pieces and give two away.)*

Do you know what I think about when I remember that story? I remember that Jesus hung between two men when He died on the cross. He didn't share candy with them. He gave His life for them, and for us, so that our sins can be forgiven and we can have life in heaven. Just thinking about that made sharing the candy seem pretty simple.

God gives us lots of tools to use to share His love. How can you use your hands to set a Christian example? *Let children respond. (Point to throat)* I am using another tool that can set a Christian example. Our voice! How can we use our voice to be a Christian example? *Let children respond.*

In His Word, God tells us why He wants us to be Christian examples to others. *Read Ephesians 5:1–2.* God helps us share His love, so others can see it shining in us. As you leave, take a candy bar to share with a friend or your family today. *Distribute candy.*

A Friend for Life Who Saves

Truth to Teach: Jesus is our Friend and Savior, who saves us from the sickness of sin.

Scripture: 1 Peter 2:24

Preparation: Ask a doctor or nurse to bring some medical items and participate as indicated. Print the text of 1 Peter 2:24 on a card for each child.

Today I am going to tell you about my friend for life, Jesus, who saves us from the sickness of sin. I have invited a friend, *(doctor's or nurse's name),* to help us. Boys and girls, are doctors our friends? How do we know doctors are our friends? *Let children respond.* That's right, they help us when we are sick.

(Name), show us some things that you use to fight sickness and disease. *Ask the health care professional to show several items—stethoscope, thermometer, etc.—and discuss how they are used. (Name),* have you ever done something that saved someone's life? Would you tell us about it? *(This does not have to be a heroic procedure, but something as simple as diagnosing a potentially lethal condition and prescribing the correct medicine or procedure to take care of it.)*

We know that *(name)* is our friend who cares about us and does his best to save us from sickness. But I know one sickness *(name)* can't cure. It is the yuckiest, deadliest disease of all—sin. And we all have it.

I made each of us a card that tells who can cure us from the deadly sickness of sin. *Read 1 Peter 2:24.* Jesus took our sickness of sin in His own body, and died on the cross in our place. Now we live a new, healthy life as God's children, and will one day live with Him in heaven. Keep your card in a place where you will see it every day, so you can remember, Jesus is a friend for life who saves you. *Distribute cards as children leave.*

Chained? Never!

Truth to Teach: God gives us His plan for salvation in His Word. He helps us read His Word, even when the devil wants us to ignore it.

Scripture: 1 John 4:9–10

Preparation: You will need a Bible, length of chain, padlock and key, and a red paper heart to fold and place in your Bible at 1 John 4:9–10. Give each child a small Bible, a Bible story book, or a card with a Bible sticker and the text of 1 John 4:9–10.

Good morning, boys and girls. This is *(hold up Bible and let children respond.)* That's right, a Bible. How many of you have your very own Bible? How many of you have a Bible at your house? Do you keep you Bible locked up? Of course not, that would be silly.

Did you know that there is someone who hates the Bible? He hates it so much, that he would like to see the Bible chained up and locked. *Wrap the chain around the Bible and padlock it.* If he could do it, he could keep us from knowing the truth about God. Who is it that hates the Bible so much? That's right, the devil.

The devil hates the Bible. He wants us to think that it is boring, stupid, and no good to read. *Show Bible.* Can anyone tell me why?

You are absolutely right. The very message the devil doesn't want us to hear is in God's Word. He doesn't want us to know about Jesus, His love, His heaven, His will. That is why the devil wants the Bible to stay locked up forever.

But God is much stronger than the devil. In fact, when God sent His Son to die and rise again, Jesus beat the devil for good. Our Bible doesn't stay chained; God opens the lock through the death and life of His Son. *Unlock chain and remove it.* And in the Bible, *(remove heart)* we find God's love in Jesus. Let me read you God's words. *Read 1 John 4:9–10.*

As we read and study God's Word, God's Holy Spirit helps us know more about Him, and our faith grows and grows. Boys and girls, don't ever let the devil put a chain around your Bible. Don't let him tell you to keep it closed, or just let it lay around, unused. Think of God's love and open it, read it, or get your mom or dad to read it to you. *Recite (or sing) the following Bible rhyme.*

The B-I-B-L-E, *(Hold up one finger for each letter.)*
Yes, that's the Book *(Open palms like a book.)*
    for me. *(Point to self.)*
I stand *(put fist into open palm)* alone
    on the Word of God, *(Open palms like a book.)*
The B-I-B-L-E. *(Hold up one finger for each letter.)*

Before you go to bed tonight, ask your parents to read God's Word (or this verse) to you. Have a great time reading God's Word. *Distribute handout.*

White Robes and Candles

Truth to Teach: Jesus is the water of life.

Scripture: Revelation 22:12–17

Preparation: Ask an older child to wear a white robe and participate as indicated. If possible, ask the child to bring the dress he/she wore when baptized.

Gift wrap a Bible in one box and a cross in another. Tie a washer to the end of a ribbon tied to a helium-filled balloon. Place the balloon in a box, close the lid, and gift wrap this box as well. You will need an empty glass, a Bible, and a baptismal candle. Order a small felt baptismal robe from Concordia Publishing House (Baptismal Garment, order no. 88-1081) for each child.

Good morning. Meet my helper, *(child's name)*. Today we are going to learn about the water of life. Listen to what God says *(read Revelation 22:17)*. Does this mean that God will give us a special glass *(hold up empty glass)* of water when we are thirsty?

Helper: No, God is not talking about a glass of water. He is talking about the real water of life—Jesus. *(To children)* Did you know that I received Jesus into my life through the waters of Baptism?

Leader: How old were you when you were baptized?

Helper: *Response.*

Leader: Where were you baptized?

Helper: *Response.*

Leader: What was so important about your Baptism?

Helper: At my Baptism, I received three gifts. The first *(unwrap Bible)* was the gift of faith. Even though I couldn't read the Bible, the Holy Spirit put faith in me so I could believe in Jesus. The second gift *(unwrap cross)* was the forgiveness of sins. Jesus washed away my sin through His death on the cross, so I could be forgiven. The third gift *(open box and let balloon pop up)* is life in heaven.

Leader: I'd say that having Jesus as my water of life is a whole lot better than having a glass of water when I am thirsty.

Helper: That's right. *Light baptismal candle.* At my Baptism, God's Spirit touched me and filled me with the light of Christ.

Leader: That's why we give a candle to people who our baptized—to help them remember that Jesus is their light. But, *(child's name)*, why are you wearing a white robe?

Helper: When I was baptized *(show dress)*, I wore this white dress. Today I am wearing a white robe to remind me that, in my Baptism, Jesus washed away all my sin and covered me with His righteousness.

Leader: I can tell that your faith in Jesus, the water of life, is growing and growing. Thanks for helping us.

Boys and girls, take a baptismal robe today and keep it where you will see it. Thank God for the gifts He gave you in your Baptism. *Distribute robes as children leave.*

Prepared for Jesus

Truth to Teach: God keeps us prepared for life in heaven by sending His Spirit to keep our hearts and minds focused on Christ.

Scripture: Matthew 24:37–44

Preparation: You will need a cross and a paper heart. You may wish to give each child an Advent devotional booklet.

Boys and girls, how many of you are in Brownies, Cub Scouts, Girl Scouts, or Boy Scouts? When I was a scout, I was taught to be prepared.

What would you check to make sure you were prepared for school? *Children might suggest lunch box, book bag, homework, pencils, etc.* What would you check to see if you were prepared for supper? *Wash hands, set table, help with meal.*

Today is the First Sunday in Advent. Advent is a time to check and see if we are prepared—for Jesus. Let's check and see what you believe about *(show cross)* Jesus. If Jesus was born in Bethlehem, say "I know that!" *Let children respond each time.* If Jesus is really God's Son, say "Of course He is." If Jesus died on the cross for your sin, say "Ouch!" If Jesus rose from the dead on Easter morning, say "Alleluia!"

Sounds like you are prepared. Where did you learn all those things? That's right. God's Holy Spirit gave you faith in Jesus when you were baptized. As you learn about Jesus at home and Sunday school and church, God's Spirit keeps your faith strong.

Let's see how you *(show heart)* love Jesus. If you love to learn about Jesus, say "B-I-B-L-E." *Let children respond each time.* If you love to talk to Jesus, fold your hands, lift them to the sky, and say, "Dear Jesus, I love you." If you love to worship Jesus, say *(or sing)* "Praise Him, Praise Him."

God's Holy Spirit keeps you prepared for Jesus. You are prepared to celebrate Jesus' birth at Christmas. You are prepared to thank God for putting faith and love for Jesus in your heart. You are prepared for Jesus to take you home to heaven one day. Read about Jesus at home this week, it's a great way to remind yourselves that God keeps you prepared. *Distribute Advent devotional books as children leave.* Let pray, Repeat after me.

Dear Lord, Help us to be prepared for this Holiday Season. And remember that Jesus is the Reason for the season

amen.

The Awesome Advent Alphabet

Truth to Teach: God helps us share our most important Christmas gift—the news that Jesus was born to be our Savior.

Scripture: Isaiah 11:1–10

Preparation: Ask an adult to interrupt your talk and get really excited about cookies. Write the letters A, B, C on three large cards. Make or buy cookies for children.

Good morning, boys and girls. Today I'm going to teach you the Advent Alphabet. In Advent, *(hold up card)* A is for Awesome, because God's love is Awesome. In Advent, *(hold up card)* B is for Birthday, because we are getting ready to celebrate the birthday of Jesus. In Advent, *(hold up card)* C is for …

Helper*(comes in and interrupts.)*: Cookies! Cookies are Awesome!

Leader: Wow! You must really like cookies. Did you come to share your cookies?

Helper*(Looking around for cookies)*: Me eat all the cookies. Me not share cookies.

Leader: Boys and girls, do you think our friend knows about Jesus? Do you think we should ask him? *Let children respond.* Here, sir. Come sit with us.

Helper: You got cookies, share with me?

Leader: We've got something better than cookies to share with you, don't we, boys and girls? You see, we were just talking about the ABC's of Advent, and we were on the letter C. In Advent, C is for …

Helper: Cookies.

Leader: Yes, we bake cookies during Advent. But, boys and girls, can you think of another word that is special at this time of the year that begins with C? *(Children are likely to say "Christmas.")*

Helper: Christmas cookies! Me like Christmas cookies!

Leader: There is an even more important word than Christmas. In Advent, C stands for Christ. *(To helper)* Do you know about Jesus Christ? *Helper shakes head no.*

Then we do have some good news for you. Christmas is much more than cookies. Christmas is all about Christ and how He shares His love for us. In fact, *(helper's name),* Jesus loves us more than you love cookies. God sent Jesus to be born on Christmas Day so that He could grow up and do something very important for us. Boys and girls, what did Jesus do? *Let children respond.* That's right. *Point to C.* Christ died on a *(point)* cross to pay for all the things we do wrong.

(Helper's name), Jesus loves you so much. He wants to share His love with you. It's a lot better than cookies.

Helper: Jesus share love with me? *(Looking sad)* Me not share cookies. Me sorry. *(Give cookie to leader.)* Me share cookies just like Jesus share love. C is for Christ, Christmas, and Christmas cookies. Me share.

Boys and girls, take a cookie from our friend as you leave. Let it remind you that Advent is a time to share Christ and His love with everyone you know. *Distribute cookies.*

Jesus Is Forever

Truth to Teach: Jesus will keep on loving and forgiving you until it is time to live with Him in heaven.

Scripture: Luke 1:26–38

Preparation: You will need a large ball of yarn with a sign tied to the end, reading "The End." Purchase a long-lasting sucker for each child.

Today we are going to help light the Advent wreath. I'll sing a song. You sing each line after me while we watch our acolyte light the Advent wreath. *Sing to the tune: Pop Goes the Weasel.*

We gather round the Advent wreath,
The children sing His praises.
Christ will reign forever more.
Light the Advent candles.

Begin unwinding the yarn. Boys and girls, some things seem to take forever. Say "forever" with me. *Continue unwinding throughout the talk.* Do any of you have chores to do? Sometimes when you are cleaning your room, or doing the dishes, it seems like that chore takes *(lead the children in saying)* forever.

How many of you think you'll get some presents for Christmas? Doesn't it seem like waiting for Christmas just takes *(together)* forever? Or sometimes, if you're tired, doesn't it seem like sitting in church takes *(together)* forever?

Be sure you are close to the end. But the chores finally get done. Christmas finally comes, and the church service ends. *Hold up the sign.* Even big balls of yarn finally come to the end. But there is one thing that will never end—Jesus and His love for us. God's Word says that Jesus will reign as our King forever and ever. He died on the cross to win us forgiveness, and rose again to give us life forever in heaven with Him.

Forever is a long time, isn't it? How long will Jesus love me? *Lead children in answering "Forever." Continue with the following questions.* How long will Jesus forgive me? When I die and go to heaven, how long will I live with Jesus?

You are right. Jesus will keep on loving and forgiving us forever. And one day, Jesus will take us to heaven to live with Him forever. If you believe that, stand up and say "Amen." *Children respond.* I believe that too. When you go home today, you can eat this long-lasting sucker. It will remind you that Jesus' love lasts forever. *Distribute suckers. Give toddlers' suckers to their parents, rather than to the children.*

Waiting

Truth to Teach: Jesus will come again to take us home to heaven.

Scripture: Micah 5:2–4

Preparation: Prepare an adult to speak from a point the children cannot see. You will need a crown, cross, shepherd costume (robe and cloth to tie around head), and crook.

Today we light the fourth candle on our Advent wreath. The time of waiting for Christmas is almost over. What are some of the things you wait for? *Let children respond.* I can remember waiting for church to be over when I was a little boy. And waiting for dinner to be ready. And waiting for school to be out.

Back in the Old Testament times, many people were waiting and waiting for God to keep His promise to send someone. People like Abraham, Moses, Isaiah, Daniel, and Ruth were waiting and waiting. Waiting on their toes *(lead children in standing up on their toes),* hoping that the day would come soon. Waiting on their knees *(kneel),* praying "Oh, come, Oh, come," so the waiting would be over. Waiting with eyes wide open *(sit and open eyes wide),* looking and looking *(put hand to forehead)* to see if someone special was coming.

Show crown. Who can tell me what the people were waiting for? That's right, they were waiting for a king to be their ruler. *Ask a child to stand and wear crown. Then ask a second child to put on the shepherd costume and stand with the crook.* And they were also waiting for a *(let children say)* shepherd to care for them and lead them. And most of all *(ask child to hold cross),* they were waiting for a Savior to save them from their sin.

Boys and girls, did the waiting end? Did the King, the Shepherd, the Savior, come? *Let children respond.* What is His name? That's right. Now, if Jesus already came at Christmas, why do we say we are still waiting for Him today?

Voice: He will come again!

Leader: *(Be sure small children aren't frightened.)* Who is that? What did you say? Are you Jesus?

Voice: No, but I am Jesus' messenger, and I'm here to tell you that Jesus is coming again.

Leader: Do you mean that Jesus is going to come and be born in a stable again, with Mary and Joseph and angels and shepherds?

Voice: No. Jesus will come again on the last day. He will come in a bright light with the sound of the trumpet. He will come again as our King. He will come as our Shepherd, to lead us to heaven. He will come as our Savior, to open heaven and let us in.

Boys and girls, Jesus is coming again! That's why we keep waiting. Jesus was born as a baby at Christmas so that He could grow to die on the cross in our place, and rise again. Now, because Jesus won forgiveness and life for us, He is in heaven, getting our homes ready. One day Jesus will come again to take us home. Now that will be a sight worth waiting for!

The Manger/Cross

Truth to Teach: Jesus was born to die on the cross for the sin of the world.

Scripture: Luke 2:1–20

Preparation: Make a manger/cross. You will need one 40″ × 6″ piece of Foamboard and two 33½″ × 6″ pieces. Using a screw and bolt, connect pieces 1 and 2 in the middle (at the 20″ mark) to form an ×. (For a less sturdy visual, use tagboard and fasten the arms with brads.) Connect the third piece to the top, right arm of the ×, as shown. Keep the screw loose enough so that you can swing this last piece down to form a cross. In carry-out boxes, package a cupcake, candle, and a birthday card for Jesus (page 64) for each child. If you wish, include cardboard pieces and paper fasteners so children can make their own manger/cross. Ask a helper to bring in a lighted birthday cake (or cupcake) at the appropriate time.

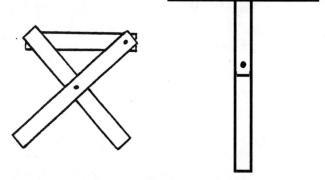

Merry Christmas! *Show manger.* Who can tell me what this looks like? That's right, it reminds us of a manger, a place where animals eat their food. I wanted to show this to you today, because we are celebrating the birth of someone who was placed in a manger. We are celebrating the birthday of *(let children respond).*

Who took care of baby Jesus while He slept in the manger? *Let children respond: Mary, Joseph, angels.* Who came to the manger to see baby Jesus? *Let children respond: the shepherds.*

That's right, Mary and Joseph and the shepherds all celebrated when baby Jesus was born. But who can tell us why God sent baby Jesus to be born? The answer is in the manger. *Turn the manger into a cross and let children respond.* That's absolutely right! Jesus was born, and slept in a *(form manger)* manger so He could give His life for our sin on the *(form cross)* cross. Then He rose again on Easter so we can live forever with Him in heaven. That makes Christmas a special celebration for us—it's the beginning of our Easter joy.

Bring out lighted cake. Let's gather around Jesus' birthday cake and sing "Happy Birthday" to Him. *Sing together, inviting the congregation to join you.* On the count of three, let's blow out the candle. 1, 2, 3. As you go back to your seats, take a Happy Birthday, Jesus kit. When you get home today, help your family celebrate the wonderful gift of Jesus. Merry Christmas! *Distribute boxes.*

You Are a Star

Truth to Teach: God's Holy Spirit helps us point others to Jesus.

Scripture: Matthew 2:1–12

Preparation: Cut out stars from yellow construction paper or cardstock. Use a marking pen to draw happy faces on the stars. Glue a star on a craft stick for each child.

Hold up a star on a stick as the children come forward. Happy Epiphany Sunday! Today we remember a story in God's Word where a star is the "star" of the story! What story am I thinking of? That's right, the story of God leading the Wise Men to see Jesus.

What was the star's job in the story? Was it supposed to sit on top of a Christmas tree? *Let children respond.* Was it supposed to show off how bright it was? Was it supposed to point the way to Jesus? You know the story! God put a special star in the sky over Bethlehem, to lead the Wise Men to find Jesus. *Hold up your star.* Can't you hear the star saying, "Over here! Jesus is over here in Bethlehem. The Savior, born to be your King! The little King you are looking for has come to save His people from their sins."

Did the star do a good job? Yes, the star led the Wise Men to Jesus. Boys and girls, there are many people today who are lost in their sin and don't know Jesus. Do you know what God asks us to do? Yes, the same job as the star. God's Holy Spirit helps us point people to Jesus. We can tell our friends that Jesus was born on Christmas so He could grow up and save them from sin by dying on the cross and rising again.

Let's play "Follow the Star." *Distribute stars.* You say *(or sing to the tune "I Am the Church")* and do my words and actions after me.

I am a star. *(Point star to self.)*
You are a star. *(Point star to a friend.)*
We are all stars together. *(Stand up and wave stars in the air.)*
All of God's children, *(Point star to several different people.)*
All across the land, *(Sweep star across "land.")*
Yes, we're God's stars forever. *(Wave star above head.)*

As you go back to your seats, wave your stars to praise Jesus and tell people how much you love Him.

The Mark

Truth to Teach: God sent His Son to die for our sin, and marks us as His children in Baptism.

Scripture: 2 Corinthians 5:20b–6:2

Preparation: Schedule the children's message after the imposition of ashes, or mark the children with the sign of the cross as they come forward. You will need a mirror. Purchase a small cross, or "Cross in My Pocket" card, for each child.

Boys and girls, it is good to be with you this Ash Wednesday. You should see yourselves. Each of you can take a look at what is on your forehead. *Hold the mirror so each child can look.* Can anyone tell us what that mark is? That's right, we have the mark of a cross on our foreheads to remind us that Jesus died on the cross.

Usually when we get smudges on us, we just look dirty. Those kind of smudges remind me of sin. Who can say some of the sins we do? *Let children respond.* We use ashes on Ash Wednesday to remind us to tell God that we are sorry for our sin.

But the smudge on your forehead today is in the shape of a cross. This isn't the first time you've had a cross on your forehead. Pastor made the sign of a cross *(make sign of cross on a child)* on your forehead, and on *(make sign of cross on a child)* your chest, when you were baptized. Jesus loves us so much that He died on the cross to take away our smudges, our sins. Beginning today, we journey with Jesus to the cross, remembering that He died for us so our sins can be forgiven.

Point to congregation. Look out there. See all the people with crosses. Today is a day to be marked with ashes, to let the whole world know that we are Christians, who believe Jesus died on the cross to win us forgiveness and eternal life.

You will have to wash off your cross before you go to bed. So I have a little cross for you. Pray with your family tonight and thank Jesus for dying on the cross for you. Carry your cross in your pocket, or in your purse, tomorrow and every day until Easter. Thank Jesus often for taking your sins away. *Distribute crosses.*

Processional

Truth to Teach: God sent His Son Jesus to save us from sin, death, and the devil.

Scripture: Matthew 21:1–9

Preparation: Use this message as the Palm Sunday processional. A week ahead of time, send a letter to each family, asking them to bring bathrobes for their children to wear in a Palm Sunday Parade. Ask volunteers to help you gather and distribute helium balloons tied with ribbons and palm branches for each child. If possible, wear a wireless microphone so you can speak as the parade is assembling. Begin by welcoming the congregation, then follow the children and any parents who wish to help to the narthex. While adults are helping the children into their bathrobes and distributing palm branches and balloons, begin telling the story. When the children are ready, lead the parade into church.

(In front of the congregation) In the name of the Father and of the Son and of the Holy Spirit. Amen. We sense a special excitement this Palm Sunday as we start our journey with Jesus through the final week of His life. His journey to the cross begins with His entrance into Jerusalem. Children, and any parents who would like to help, walk to the back of the church with me. Let's remember what happened on that very first Palm Sunday.

Tell the story from the Gospel, being sure the congregation can hear you, as you lead the children out, help them get into their robes, and distribute palm branches and balloons. As you finish the story, lead the children to the door for the processional. Tell the children to shout "Hosanna" every time you shout it, and to hold onto their balloons until you give the signal.

(From the back of the church) Boys and girls, please repeat each phrase of this prayer after me. These palms remind us/that Jesus came to Jerusalem,/to die on a cross/for our sin./Bless us who carry them/in honor of Jesus, our King./Amen. Raise your palms and let's follow the cross!

Lead the children to the front of the church as the congregation sings the processional hymn. Shout "Hosanna" many times, encouraging the children to shout after you, and wave their palms.

Gather the children at the altar.

(When the hymn is ended) Thank you for helping us with our Palm Sunday Parade. Now say "Hosanna" with me three times. On the third hosanna, let go of your balloons. Hosanna! Hosanna! Hosanna! *Release balloons.*

As you return to your seats, wave your palm branches in celebration of our King, Jesus.

From Thorns to Glory

Truth to Teach: Jesus died and rose to take the sting out of death and win us a crown of life.

Scripture: 1 Corinthians 15:55–56; Revelation 2:10

Preparation: Wrap thorns around a grapevine wreath. Ask an adult helper to wear an Easter hat, ball cap, and a policeman's (or some other type) of hat. Purchase silver and gold baby's-breath, or similar decorations, to wrap around the wreath during the talk. Make a Foamboard or tagboard crown to nestle in the baby's-breath. Be sure the crown includes a yellow, red, and green jewel. Make a cloth or paper banner to pull out of the crown. It should read: "I will give you a crown of life." Make a Crown of Life Kit for each child: Place a small straw wreath (purchased at a craft store) in a plastic bag for each child. Include the Crown of Life pattern (page 64) and a strip of colored paper reading, "I will give you a crown of life." You may want to have the choir or a soloist softly sing "Jesus Loves Me, This I Know" as you describe the crown of thorns, and "His Banner over Me Is Love" as you pull the banner from the crown. You will need a Bible.

Happy Easter, boys and girls. Do you see some people wearing special hats today? *(Helper's name)* is wearing her Easter hat. Did you know that Jesus is going to give you a very special Easter hat—one He paid for? Let me show you what I mean.

Helper puts on baseball cap. Who would wear this hat? *Let children respond each time. Helper puts on second hat.* Who would wear this kind of hat? *Hold up crown of thorns.* Who wore this hat? Yes, Jesus wore this hat—a crown of thorns—just for us. Because He loves us so much, Jesus let the thorns sink into His head. Ouch, the sting of sin! He let nails pierce His hands and feet. Ouch, the sting of sin! He let a spear go into His side. Ouch, the sting of sin! Jesus died and His friends put His body into a grave—ouch, the sting of sin—so we can have a special Easter hat.

Let me show you what your Easter hat may look like. *Wrap baby's-breath and other decorations over the thorns.* I have covered the thorns with silver and gold to remind us how beautiful heaven will be. Because Jesus died on the cross to take our sin away, we will get to live with Him in heaven one day. *Nestle the crown in the baby's-breath.* This crown reminds us that we are children of the King, and one day we will live with our King in heaven. *Point to jewels.* The red jewel reminds us that Jesus shed His blood for our sin. The yellow jewel reminds that Jesus rose on Easter morning. The green jewel reminds us that we will live forever. Now you know—Jesus wore a crown of thorns so that one day He can give us a Crown of Life in heaven. *Pull the banner from the midst of the crown and read it to the children.*

Do you like my Crown of Life—my Easter hat? *Point to children.* I can see how special each of you are going to look. People who are getting a Crown of Life don't have to be afraid of sin or the devil. They don't have to be afraid of death. Listen to God's Word. *Read 1 Corinthians 15:55–56.* Jesus has taken the sting out of death. Thanks to be to God for giving us the victory and promising us a Crown of Life! To help you celebrate, I am going to give each of you a Crown of Life Kit. Ask your family to help you make a crown, and thank Jesus for winning us a home in heaven.

Looking for Jesus

Truth to Teach: God sent His Son Jesus to die for us and rise again, making us Easter People, bound for heaven.

Scripture: Mark 16:1–7

Preparation: Make or purchase a large white kite. Write "He Is Risen" on the sail. Add a long tail. If possible, use fishing line and a system of pullies to raise the kite over (or out of) the baptismal font during the talk. If that is not possible have a helper hold the kite by the font. Hang a pall (cloth) over a frame or box large enough for the children to walk through. Practice the talk with your professional team and organist. Place a small Easter treat in a plastic egg for each child. It works well to use this talk as the Gospel Processional.

Boys and girls, it's Easter morning. Let's go for an Easter walk to find Jesus. We have music *(Easter hymn introduction begins),* and the processional cross and candles *(crucifer and torch bearers join you),* so let's go. What should we visit first on our Easter walk? Let's follow the cross and find out.

Lead the children around the church as the congregation sings the first stanza. Stop by your altar cross or a specially-placed Easter cross. I should have known—the empty cross. Boys and girls, the Easter cross *(point to cross)* is an empty cross. It is empty because Jesus didn't stay dead on the cross. His friends took Him down after He had died for our sins. I wonder where we will go next.

Lead the children as the congregation sings. Stop at the pall. Look at this beautiful blanket. It is called a funeral pall. It covers the casket—the box where the body of someone who has died is placed—at funerals in our church. Instead of putting Jesus in a casket, His friends put Him in a cave, called a tomb. Do you think Jesus will be inside the grave? Let's find out. *Have torchbearers lift the pall as you and the children walk through. The congregation sings the next stanza.*

Well, did we find Jesus' body? *Let children respond.* Why not? *Let children respond.* Are you sure? Then let's tell the whole world *(point to kite as it rises),* He is risen! *Repeat several times so children are shouting—He is what? He is risen!—as you lead them to the baptismal font.* Why are we stopping at the baptismal font on our Easter Walk? It is here that we were made Easter People. God's Holy Spirit gave us the faith to believe that Jesus died for us and rose again, so that we can be Easter People and live with Him.

Boys and girls, the last stop on our Easter walk will be in the middle of the people of God. *Continue the procession into the middle of the congregation and read the Gospel for the day.*

Boys and girls, you are Easter People. Jesus is risen and lives in you. Take an Easter surprise to help you remember our Easter Walk. *Distribute eggs.*

Unbelievable!

Truth to Teach: God gives us His Holy Spirit to help us understand that our faith in Jesus is the most important thing we have.

Scripture: John 20:18–31

Preparation: A box with a live rabbit.

Display box. What do your think is inside my box? A Bible? A cross? If I told you a live rabbit was in here, would you believe me? What would it take to convince you? If you saw the rabbit, would you believe me?

Show the rabbit. When the rabbit was in the box, some of you believed me and some of you didn't. Now, because you see it, all of you believe me. One of Jesus' disciples, Thomas, had a hard time believing that Jesus had really risen from the dead. He said, "I won't believe it until I see the wounds in Jesus' hands and feet and side."

Boys and girls, how many of you believe that on Good Friday, Jesus died on the cross to take away our sins? Raise your hands. Were you there? Did you see it? Yet you believe it. That's because God's Holy Spirit gives you faith. I believe it too.

How many of you believe that Jesus' friends put His body into a grave, but on the third day, Jesus rose from the dead? Raise your hands. Were you there? Did you see it? Yet you believe it. I do too.

How many of you believe that, when you die, you will go to heaven to live with Jesus? Raise your hands. Have you been there? Yet you believe.

Boys and girls, believing that Jesus died for us and rose again is the most important thing we can ever know. God gave us the gift of faith at our Baptism. His Holy Spirit will keep you believing.

Share God's Love

Truth to Teach: God helps us live out our faith, so others will "know we are Christians by our love."

Scripture: John 13:34–35

Preparation: Write the three messages in the talk on three small pieces of paper. Roll them up and place them in three separate balloons. Blow up the balloons and tie them. Write the following words with permanent marking pen on three more uninflated balloons: care, forgive, gifts. You will need a pin to pop the inflated balloons with rolled-up messages; three pictures: a picture of your mother, of Jesus, and of someone using God-given talents; a Bible; an inexpensive picture frame for each child.

6 balloons

Boys and girls, God loves us, right? *Show inflated balloons.* Inside these balloons are ways God shows His love. Who wants to pop one? *Choose a child and help him handle the pin.* The paper inside *(message 1)* says, "We know God loves us because He gave us great people like grandmas and moms, sisters and aunts, who help us and care for us. *Ask a child to hold up the picture of your mother.* This is a picture of my mom. She cared for me and helped me and taught me about Jesus. *Ask a child to pop the second balloon. Take out message 2.* We know God loves us because, "He forgives us, even when we make big mistakes." Boy, I have made some big mistakes. How about you? *Let children respond.* I brought a picture of God's Son, Jesus *(ask child to hold picture up).* God sent Jesus to die on the cross, and rise again on Easter, so our sin can be forgiven. God really loves us.

We know God loves us because … *Ask a child to pop the third balloon. Remove message 3.* The last message says, "God gives us abilities such as coloring, running, reading, and hitting a ball." Who is good at coloring? *Let children raise hands.* Running? Reading? Hitting a ball? God really shows us He loves us by giving us our talents and abilities. *Ask child to hold third picture.* Here is a picture of teens who are using their talents on a servant event.

God shows His love by *(point to first picture)* giving us people who care, forgiving us and planning a home in heaven for us *(show picture of Jesus),* and by giving us abilities to use *(point to last picture).* But God doesn't want us to keep His love all to ourselves. He says *(read from Bible),* "A new command I give you: Love one another. As I have loved you, so you must love one another. By this all men will know that you are My disciples, if you love one another."

God helps us share His love by *(blow up and knot balloon with "care" written on it)* caring for others. *Hug a child as you give her the balloon to hold.* We share God's love by *(blow up the balloon with "forgive")* forgiving those who sin against us. *Give the balloon to a child and say, "I'm sorry."* And we share God's loves by *(blow up balloon with "gifts")* using our gifts and talents to help other people. *Hand balloon to child and say, "I blew this up just for you."*

Let's show our moms and everyone else that we are Christians, by sharing God's love. As you leave, take a picture frame. Put a picture of yourself, or draw one, in the frame that shows a way you can share God's love. Give the picture to your mom, or someone else who is special to you. *Distribute picture frames.*

Be Bold

Truth to Teach: God's Holy Spirit gives us the power to be bold for Jesus.

Scripture: Acts 2:14a, 22–32

Preparation: Prepare an older child to come forward dressed in a sports uniform, carrying equipment, and participate in the dialog as indicated. You will need three signs reading "I love Jesus." Sign 1 should be small and written with pencil. Sign 2 should be larger and written with a thin-tip marking pen. Sign 3 should be very large and written in bright, bold letters. Have an "I love Jesus" button or sticker for each child.

Boys and girls, God promises to give us His Holy Spirit to help us be bold for Jesus. I have some signs to show you. *Have three children hold up the signs.* Let's say I want to hold one of these signs when I walk into McDonald's. Which one would tell others most strongly that I love Jesus? *Let children respond.*

To be bold for Jesus means we aren't shy about letting people know why we love Jesus. We love Him because *(let children respond).* That's right. Jesus loves us so much. He took the punishment for our sin by dying on the cross. Then Jesus rose again to win us new life with Him. Before Jesus went back to heaven to get our homes ready, He promised to send us His Holy Spirit to make us bold to share His love.

Have any of you ever actually worn a sign into McDonald's that says, "I love Jesus"? I haven't either. But many of our words and actions do tell people how bold our love for Jesus is. Let me show you what I mean.

I've invited *(name of child in uniform, with sports equipment)* to help me. Let's pretend I'm her coach. Listen to what *(child's name)* says and tell me if her words are like *(point to each sign)* the small sign, the medium sign, or the great big sign.

Coach: *(Child's name),* we have a game next Sunday morning. You'll have to be at the ballpark at *(the time of your church service).* You'll be there, won't you?

Child: I guess it won't hurt to miss church one Sunday. Sure, I can make it.

Boys and girls, which sign is she wearing? *Let children respond.* Let's try it again. *Repeat your dialog. Child replies, "I don't think my dad would let me miss church. I would like to play, but I don't want my dad to get mad."* Now which sign is she wearing? *Let children respond.*

Let's try it one more time. *Repeat your dialog. This time the child responds, "I can be there at (a time shortly after your church service), Coach. But I want to go to church and Sunday school first. The team is important, but Jesus comes first. By the way, do you want to come with me?"* Now which sign is she wearing? *Let children respond.*

Boys and girls, God's Holy Spirit will help you be bold for Jesus in what you say and do. Take a Jesus button to wear today. Be bold for Jesus! *Distribute buttons as children leave.*

The Trinity in Color

Truth to Teach: Our God is Three in One. God the Father created and cares for us; God the Son died and rose again to save us; God the Holy Spirit gifts us with faith and helps us grow as God's children.

Scripture: Matthew 3:13–17

Preparation: Make a crepe paper flag for each child. Cut 18″ strips of blue, red, and white crepe paper. Glue a straw in the middle of each strip. Cut a large ring or hoop out of cardboard. Write the word "Father" on a piece of blue construction paper and tape it to the hoop; attach "Son" (red paper); and "Holy Spirit" (white paper).

Hand out the flags as the children come forward. Boys and girls, do you know that a name for our God is "Trinity"? That's right. Our God is called the Trinity. Trinity means "three-in-one"—one God, but three persons.

Point to "Father" on the hoop. This is God the Father. True blue stands for our Father because He created you, and no promise does He undo. *Point to the Son.* Red is for God the Son, for through His death, heaven for us He won. *Point to the Holy Spirit.* White is for the Holy Spirit, for through the Holy Spirit, new life we inherit.

Each of you has a colored flag. If you have a blue flag, wave it. *Demonstrate waving a blue flag.* Blue is for God the Father. From now on, whenever I say Father, wave it to praise God the Father.

If you have a red flag, wave it. Red is for God the *(let children respond).* When I say Son, wave your flag to praise God the Son.

If you have a white flag, wave it. White is for God the *(let children respond).* When I say Holy Spirit, wave your flag to praise God the Holy Spirit.

If I say "three-in-one," that means all of you. From now on, when I say three-in-one, all of you wave your flags.

Hold the hoop and point to the cards as you speak. Boys and girls, I love the Father because He made me. Did the blue flags wave? I love His Son Jesus because He saved me. Did the red flags wave? I love the Holy Spirit because He helps me live as God's child. Did the white flags wave? I love God, the Three-in-One, because He loves me.

Sing a song or hymn containing the three names of the Trinity. Ask the congregation to sing along, and lead the children in waving their flags at the right time.

Boys and girls, during the rest of the service, whenever you hear Father, Son, or Spirit—wave the correctly-colored flag. When you hear "Three-in-One" or "Trinity," all of you wave your flags. Happy Trinity Sunday!

Psalm 23

The LORD is my shepherd, I shall not
be in want.
He makes me lie down in green
pastures,
He leads me beside quiet waters,
He restores my soul.
He guides me in paths of
righteousness
for His name's sake.
Psalm 23:1–3

Luther's Morning Prayer

I thank Thee, my heavenly Father, through Jesus Christ, Thy dear Son, that Thou hast kept me this night from all harm and danger; and I pray Thee that Thou wouldst keep me this day also from sin and every evil, that all my doings and life may please Thee. For into Thy hands I commend myself, my body and soul, and all things. Let Thy holy angel be with me that the wicked foe may have no power over me. Amen.

Quake Calmer Kit

GOD'S PROMISES

LORD, THANK YOU FOR ANGELS WATCHING OVER ME, 'CAUSE SOMETIMES I GET SCARED AS SCARED CAN BE! BUT THEN I REMEMBER JUST WHAT YOU HAVE SAID, AND THINK OF ANGELS PROTECTING ME FROM MY TOES TO MY HEAD! I'M GLAD THEY ARE WITH ME NIGHT AND DAY, GUIDING AND PROTECTING ALONG LIFE'S WAY. AMEN.

Bible Presentation Outline

Send a letter stating the date and time of the presentation to the home of each child who will receive a Bible. Include a copy of the following reading so families will know what to expect. Make follow-up phone calls to answer parents' questions and invite them personally to attend. If you give the Bibles out at the end of a children's message, invite the parents forward and ask their children to stand with them. Children who will not be receiving a Bible may watch, and look forward to the day they will get one.

The Presentation of Bibles

Leader: God made us His children in our Baptism. We promised, through our sponsors and parents, to grow in faith through the reading of His Word. As our children were baptized, we promised to place the Holy Scriptures into their hands, and ask the Holy Spirit to help them grow in faith and love for Jesus. Are you willing to carry out this promise?

Parents: Yes, we are committed to our promise to help our children grow in faith, and in love for God and His ways.

Leader: Then place the Holy Bible into the hands of your child and share a word about its importance and the Good News of Jesus revealed in it. *(Let parents talk to their children.)*

Leader: Parents, help your children read their Bible and grow to love it. Through the power of the Holy Spirit, may the Scriptures be a blessing in the faith life of your child and your home. Children, will you read your Bibles and share the love of Jesus with your families? If so, say "Yes, with Jesus' help."

Children: Yes, with Jesus' help.

Leader: Go in peace, dedicated to growing in the knowledge of God's grace and salvation, through the study of His Word.

Birthday Card for Jesus

Crown of Life Pattern

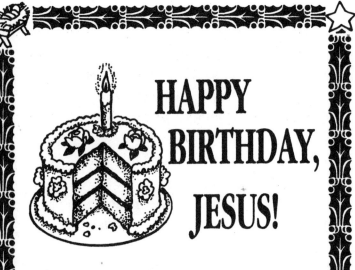

HAPPY BIRTHDAY, JESUS!

Put the candle on your cupcake. Ask your parents to help you light the candle. Sing " Happy Birthday" to Jesus.

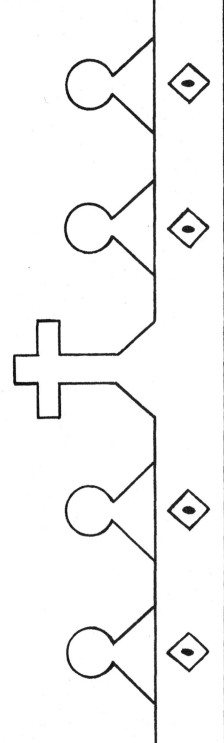